RACISM IN MODERN RUSSIA

D0140236

Russian Shorts

Russian Shorts is a series of thought-provoking books published in a slim format. The Shorts books examine key concepts, personalities, and moments in Russian historical and cultural studies, encompassing its vast diversity from the origins of the Kievan state to Putin's Russia. Each book is intended for a broad range of readers, covers a side of Russian history and culture that has not been well understood, and is meant to stimulate conversation.

Series Editors:

Eugene M. Avrutin, Professor of Modern European Jewish History, University of Illinois, USA

Stephen M. Norris, Professor of History, Miami University, USA

Editorial Board:

Edyta Bojanowska, Professor of Slavic Languages and Literatures, Yale University, USA

Ekaterina Boltunova, Associate Professor of History, Higher School of Economics, Russia

Eliot Borenstein, Professor of Russian and Slavic, New York University, USA

Melissa Caldwell, Professor of Anthropology, University of California Santa Cruz, USA

Choi Chatterjee, Professor of History, California State University, Los Angeles, USA

Robert Crews, Professor of History, Stanford University, USA

Dan Healey, Professor of Modern Russian History, University of Oxford, UK

Polly Jones, Associate Professor of Russian, University of Oxford, UK

Paul R. Josephson, Professor of History, Colby College, USA

Marlene Laruelle, Research Professor of International Affairs, George Washington University, USA

Marina Mogilner, Associate Professor, University of Illinois at Chicago, USA

Willard Sunderland, Henry R. Winkler Professor of Modern History, University of Cincinnati, USA

Published Titles

Pussy Riot: Speaking Punk to Power, Eliot Borenstein

Memory Politics and the Russian Civil War: Reds Versus Whites, Marlene Laruelle and Margarita Karnysheva

Russian Utopia: A Century of Revolutionary Possibilities, Mark Steinberg

Racism in Modern Russia: From the Romanovs to Putin, Eugene M. Avrutin

Upcoming Titles

Art, History and the Making of Russian National Identity: Vasily Surkiov, Viktor Vasnetsov, and the Remaking of the Past, Stephen M. Norris

Russia and the Jewish Question: A Modern History, Robert Weinberg

The Soviet Gulag: History and Memory, Jeffrey S. Hardy

The Afterlife of the 'Soviet Man': Rethinking Homo Sovieticus, Gulnaz Sharafutdinova

The Multiethnic Soviet Union and its Demise, Brigid O'Keeffe

Russian Food since 1800: Empire at Table, Catriona Kelly

Meanwhile, In Russia: Russian Memes and Viral Video Culture, Eliot Borenstein

A Social History of the Russian Army, Roger R. Reese

Why We Need Russian Literature, Angela Brintlinger

Nuclear Russia, Paul Josephson

Eugene M. Avrutin is the Tobor Family Endowed Professor of Modern European Jewish History at the University of Illinois, Urbana-Champaign. He is the author and co-editor of several award-winning books, including *Jews and the Imperial State: Identification Politics in Tsarist Russia* (2010) and *The Velizh Affair: Blood Libel in a Russian Town* (2018). Most recently, he edited, with Elissa Bemporad, *Pogroms: A Documentary History* (2021).

RACISM IN MODERN RUSSIA

FROM THE ROMANOVS TO PUTIN

Eugene M. Avrutin

BLOOMSBURY ACADEMIC
LONDON • NEW YORK • OXFORD • NEW DELHI • SYDNEY

BLOOMSBURY ACADEMIC
Bloomsbury Publishing Plc
50 Bedford Square, London, WC1B 3DP, UK
1385 Broadway, New York, NY 10018, USA
29 Earlsfort Terrace, Dublin 2, Ireland

BLOOMSBURY, BLOOMSBURY ACADEMIC and the Diana logo are trademarks of Bloomsbury
Publishing Plc

First published in Great Britain 2022

Series design by Tjaša Krivec

Cover image: Antisemitic postcard depicting critters with human heads crawling around the globe.
© The Blavatnik Archive

A catalogue record for this book is available from the British Library.

Library of Congress Cataloging-in-Publication Data
Names: Avrutin, Eugene M., author.
Title: Racism in modern Russia : from the Romanovs to Putin / Eugene M. Avrutin.
Description: London ; New York : Bloomsbury Academic, 2022. | Series: Russian shorts | Includes
bibliographical references and index.
Identifiers: LCCN 2021036444 (print) | LCCN 2021036445 (ebook) | ISBN 9781350097285 (pb) |
ISBN 9781350097278 (hb) | ISBN 9781350097292 (epdf) | ISBN 9781350097315 (ebook)
Subjects: LCSH: Racism–Russia (Federation)–History. | Russia (Federation)–Race relations–History. |
Anti-racism–Soviet Union. | Soviet Union–Race relations.
Classification: LCC DK510.33 .A933 2022 (print) | LCC DK510.33 (ebook) | DDC 305.800947–dc23
LC record available at https://lccn.loc.gov/2021036444
LC ebook record available at https://lccn.loc.gov/2021036445

ISBN: HB: 978-1-3500-9727-8
PB: 978-1-3500-9728-5
ePDF: 978-1-3500-9729-2
eBook: 978-1-3500-9731-5

Typeset by Deanta Global Publishing Services, Chennai, India
Printed and bound in Great Britain

To find out more about our authors and books visit www.bloomsbury.com and sign up for our
newsletters.

To Yingying

CONTENTS

FIGURES

ACKNOWLEDGMENTS

The idea of writing a short book on the long history of racism came to me in the fall of 2016, just as the events surrounding the US presidential election took a series of unexpected turns. For the past century, the overwhelming majority of Jews in America have voted for the Democratic Party, even as other Americans, with similar achievement of social status and levels of education, have consistently supported the Republican camp. But this was not the case for a small slice of the Jewish community, the Russian-speaking Soviet and Russian immigrants who, since their arrival in America in the 1970s, have staunchly identified with the Republican Party's narrative of self-reliance, opposition to the welfare state, and aversion to "socialism."

This part of the story I was familiar with, of course. But in the fall of 2016 one thing I couldn't come to terms with was how an entire community of people I had known since I was a little boy (the kids with whom I played basketball and baseball in Houston, Texas, to say nothing of my own family members) could throw their allegiance behind a man with a strong commitment for blatant falsehoods, deep aversion for human decency, and overt support for white supremacy and misogyny. What was it about Donald Trump that drew so many Russian Jews to vote for an openly xenophobic candidate? Did Trump truly embody the American Dream, with his deep infatuation for glamorous women and shiny objects? How could respectable professionals—children of Holocaust survivors no less—call themselves white nationalists and proud believers in the alt-right? And why weren't more Russian–Jewish immigrants horrified when white supremacists marched in Charlottesville in August 2017, chanting "Jews will not replace us," or at the mass shooting at the Tree of Life synagogue in Pittsburgh in October 2018? Perhaps Gary Shteyngart, the Soviet-born American writer, was on to something when he suggested that Trump's frank-talking racism made Russian immigrants secure in their own sense of whiteness?[1]

I am fortunate to have found a group of friends and colleagues who offered their wisdom and provided encouragement as I worked on the project. I would like to say a special thank you to Rhodri Mogford for supporting the idea of doing a Shorts series in Russian history and culture and to Steve Norris for his efforts in making the book series a success. I presented portions of the project at the conference on "Rethinking Violence in Jewish History" at Stanford University and at the conference on "Thinking 'Race' in the Russian and Soviet Empires" at the University of Illinois at Chicago and the University of Chicago. I am grateful to Charles Steinwedel's perceptive response at the Chicago conference. I benefited from the discussion at the Carolina Russia Seminar, and owe a special thanks to Eren Tasar for the invitation. I finally mustered the courage to present a chapter-in-progress at the Illinois History workshop. My thanks to Dana Rabin, Ken Cuno, Marc Hertzman, and Mark Steinberg for asking challenging questions. Kevin Mumford provided encouragement at just the right time. Eileen Kane, Steve Norris, Marina Mogilner, and two external readers read the entire manuscript and offered numerous constructive comments and pointed criticisms, pushing me to rework some of my initial formulations.

For their support over the years, I am grateful to Elissa Bemporad, David Shneer, z"l, Gennady Estraikh, Robert Weinberg, Harriet Murav, and Jeff Veidlinger. The Tobor Family Endowment, as well as a grant from the Research Board of the University of Illinois, provided financial assistance for research. I owe a debt of gratitude to Franziska Yost for research assistance and Joseph Lenkart of the Slavic Reference Service at the University of Illinois for expert advice.

This was a difficult book to write on several levels. It went through multiple revisions. I wrote the bulk of the manuscript in isolation during an unprecedented public health crisis, without direct access to libraries or archives. I could not have completed the project without the companionship of my family, Abi and Yingying, for which I am particularly grateful.

INTRODUCTION

The Western Biriulëvo district sits on the southernmost tip of Moscow. It has no metro stop. Only a highway connects the district with the rest of the capital. Surrounded by railroads, giant cooling towers from a local thermal plant, rundown factories, and dozens of market and vegetable warehouses, Biriulëvo offers some of the cheapest housing in the nation's capital. After the breakup of the Soviet Union, the district witnessed an uptick in labor migration, mainly from the Caucasus and Central Asia, and acquired a reputation as a remote and seedy part of Moscow. One local resident described the place as a "sewer, Moscow's sewer, where the government [stores] all the waste."[1]

Orhan Zeinalov, an Azerbaijani man, had left Baku in search of work. Like many migrant workers, he eventually found a job at the wholesale vegetable warehouse in the Western Biriulëvo district and rented a cheap room nearby in a high-rise apartment block. On October 15, 2013, the Russian police arrested the thirty-year-old Zeinalov, charging him with killing Yegor Shcherbakov, a twenty-five-year-old white ethnic Russian man. Shcherbakov and his girlfriend, Ksenia Popova, had been walking home three days earlier. Just as the pair approached the entrance to their apartment building, Zeinalov insulted Popova. It remains unclear what was said, but it did not take long for tensions to escalate. The men got into a heated shouting match, at which time Zeinalov pulled out a knife and stabbed Shcherbakov to death in front of his girlfriend.

The murder of Yegor Shcherbakov triggered a large riot. The event, captured dramatically on homemade videos, received international attention in the press. On Sunday October 13, disgruntled local residents, armed with sticks, rocks, and pickaxes, marched to the Biriuza shopping center. They proceeded to smash windows and loot goods before turning their attention to the warehouse in search of dark-skinned workers. When night approached, the protestors threw beer bottles at police officers, rolled over several minibuses, and destroyed fruit stalls. The police wound up arresting 380 individuals for vandalism but released most of them within twenty-four hours. Subsequently, the interior minister ordered a crackdown on illegal migrants. Around 1,200 warehouse workers, most of whom were from the Caucasus or Central Asia, were arrested.[2]

The Biriulëvo disturbance turned out to be one of the largest outbreaks of anti-migrant unrest in Putin's Russia. One local resident, in justification of the violence, said, "We've had it up to here with these blacks."[3] Clashes and arrests continued late into the night. The crowd that descended on the shopping center was comprised of men in their twenties and thirties, including right-wing nationalists wearing dark clothing, but older men and women and the occasional mother strolling a baby carriage with a camera in hand joined the demonstration, as well. Some in the crowd, which grew to several thousand people, could be

Image 0.1 People leaving a shopping center vandalized during a riot in the southern Biriulëvo district of Moscow, on October 13, 2013. Residents took part in the riot, bashing in the doors and windows of the shopping center and beating up security guards in a protest sparked by a murder blamed on an Azerbaijani migrant. © Courtesy of AFP Photo via Getty Images.

heard chanting, "Russia for the Russians," with their animus directed toward dark-skinned migrants.[4] For a growing number of people in the Russian Federation, the slogan became a nationalistic rallying cry. Russian print media, along with the state-aligned television channels, stoked hostilities by describing Central Asian and Caucasian migrants as "illegals" (*nelegaly*), "guest workers" (*gastarbeitery*), and other charged labels. Surveys conducted by the Levada Center revealed that a majority of the respondents agreed that Russia belonged to ethnic— that is to say, white European—Russians, while almost two-thirds supported firmer immigration restrictions and believed in the folk tale that migrants contributed to a rise in crime.[5]

The slogan "Russia for the Russians" is not a recent invention. It first gained notoriety in the very last years of the tsarist regime, appealing primarily to individuals drawn to the radical right: a politically diverse and not always coherent ideological movement obsessed with Russia's imminent decline. Activists chanting the slogan perceived the old order as under attack. Russian rulers—from Tsar Alexander III (1881–94) to Vladimir Putin (2000-)—spent a great deal of resources trying to control territories far removed from the center of power. In late imperial Russia, as in Putin's time, a series of crises in the borderlands threatened the sovereignty of Russian statehood and, by extension, the strength and security of the Russian people. The idea was to protect the nation by drawing exclusionary boundaries between ethnic Russians and populations in the distant borderlands—Chinese and Koreans in the east, Jews and Poles in the west, and, in the Soviet and post-Soviet periods, migrants from the southern peripheries of Central Asia and the Caucasus—who allegedly posed a threat to the established ethnographic order.

Organized chronologically in four concise chapters, spanning approximately 150 years, *Racism in Modern Russia* moves beyond the history of ideas to explore a dynamic process known as racialization: how racist attitudes and perceptions of inferiority constructed a hierarchy of human difference in day-to-day experiences. Race provides a window onto the messy world of inequality and privilege, denigration and belonging, and power and policy. Focusing on several key moments in modern Russian history, this book probes the ways in which fixed

Image 0.2 Anti-Semitic postcard depicting critters with human heads crawling around the globe, stating: "The kikes crawl around, Generating misfortune, We will need to build huts for them, With the devil's poison." The extreme-right slogan "Russia for the Russians" appears on the top left corner of the postcard. © Courtesy of the Blavatnik Archive.

markers of difference—including skin color—created exclusionary boundaries in everyday life. Race, in other words, is not only about the history of ideas or legal policies; it is also about the creation and maintenance of ineradicable boundaries in a social system.[6]

Before the early 2000s, scholars of Russian history and culture have overwhelmingly dismissed the wider impact of race-based thought and practices.[7] What factors account for this silence? Why have scholars shown so little interest in historical and theoretical discussions of race? Over the course of 150 years, so the argument goes, Russian administrators failed to establish a racial regime based explicitly on biological theories of human development. They never imposed absolute hierarchies, controlled populations, or limited citizenship rights based on blood or skin color. Race did not appear as an official category in censuses, passports, and other state-issued documents, as did *sosloviia* (social estates) in imperial Russia or class (social position) and nationality in the Soviet Union. For long stretches of time, at least until the late- nineteenth century, religion served as the most basic category of identity for Russia's subjects.

Some scholars have maintained that Russia's long-established tolerance of confessional diversity, as well as its flexibility to govern the varied circumstances of empire, shielded it from racism. Russia's colonial expansion played an important role in the construction of tolerant attitudes toward minority groups. Unlike its British or French counterparts, Russia was a contiguous empire. As it expanded its territories and acquired populations, absolute distinctions did not surface between the center and periphery and the "us" and "them." In contrast to overseas empires, according to this scholarship, Russia's elites did not express fears of miscegenation, the moral and sexual dangers of contamination, and the destabilization of the fixed category of Russianness. The global dimensions of the color line—what W. E. B. Du Bois famously called the "relation of the darker to the lighter races of men in Africa and Asia, in America and the islands of the sea"— did not seem to apply to Russia.[8] The autocracy's active promotion of religiosity for all faiths of the empire—the so-called toleration thesis— helps to explain why Russians did not develop the racist thinking that became so pervasive in nineteenth-century Europe and beyond.[9]

Soviet Russia, at first glance, also seems to sit outside the orbit of the overtly racist regime. The 1917 Revolution promoted a social utopia premised on equality and internationalism. Newspapers and other propaganda organs highlighted the Soviet Union's anti-racist image on the world stage. Anthropologists and ethnographers studied race formation not in terms of biology, but in terms of sociohistorical processes. Soviet policy celebrated ethnic mixing, even as it called for all individuals to have only one officially recognized national identity. The idea was to destroy national traditions and to ease ethnic tensions. Intermarriage was deemed the surest way of creating a single Soviet people. Soviet leaders went out of their way to denounce the United States for its racism, while showcasing the USSR as a society where such practices were absent. African American writers such as Langston Hughes, Claude McKay, and Du Bois looked to the Soviet Union as a model for Black equality.[10]

This book conceptualizes the color line as inherently messy. Racialization was never a fixed or stable process. The development of hierarchical boundaries and exclusionary practices operated in a multilayered landscape. By the end of the nineteenth century, a dizzying array of ethno-racial groups resided in the Russian Empire, a contiguous landmass that extended from the Baltic and Black Seas to the Siberian fur-bearing regions, the Kazakh Steppe, and Central Asia. In this highly variegated landscape, ethnic Russians comprised less than half of the total population.[11] Anthropologists studied a diverse landscape of racial types, categorizing populations by an assortment of indicators such as hair and eye color, height, chest circumference, length of legs and head, skull measurements, and nasal indices. In their taxonomies, they described everyone from Great Russians, Little Russians, Poles, and Jews to Georgians, Caucasian native types, and the yellow peoples of the Far East.[12] A visitor who walked the streets of Moscow, St. Petersburg, Kazan, or Odessa would see what one historian characterized as "an alphabet soup of people at all stages of human development from the most benighted and primitive 'children of nature' to the most sophisticated, urbane European gentleman."[13]

Not everyone's skin was white. And color—with limited exceptions—did not determine social position or citizenship rights in either imperial Russia or the Soviet Union. The occasional Black women and men who paid a visit were rarely judged by their skin.[14] Nevertheless, group prejudices—based on anatomical characteristics and also the much harder to pin-down cultural attributes—played a fundamental role in creating absolute hierarchies and divisions in everyday life. Occasionally, the designations took an unexpected turn. A case in point is the role of forced labor. By the eighteenth century, Russia had developed a well-established system of human bondage akin to American slavery. Serfdom meant not only the prohibition of the right of movement, but also the total control of the body. Serfs endured countless rituals of subordination, whippings, and degradations. Russians described the status of serfdom as *rabstvo*—or slavery—the same word that was used to refer to the American institution. Russians were convinced of the inherent inferiority of serfs. But they did not use skin color to legitimize the system of bondage or invent highly elaborate scientific racial arguments—based on brain sizes, respiratory systems, and numerous other physiological differences—to justify the institution.[15]

In contrast to slaves in America, serfs could not be physically distinguished from their masters by their skin. Nor were they complete outsiders, deposited against their will in a foreign land. To be sure, Russians often labeled serfs as intrinsically lazy, childlike, and ignorant. But because there were no visible racial distinctions between owner and owned, after the emancipation of serfs in 1861—the majority of whom were ethnic Russians—their freedom did not pose the same threat as that of the emancipated Black slave in the United States.[16] One of the long-term consequences of this historical reality is that, as former serfs blended into the Russian core, certain other populations who "looked" and "behaved" differently were marginalized as visibly distinct groups.

Over the long span of Russian history, classificatory systems played an important role in labeling people. Passports and other documentary records provided authorities a powerful tool to make sense of a diverse population. From the tsarist era to the fall of the Soviet Union, all individuals were categorized according to a state-ascribed collective identity. In Tsarist Russia, individuals were classified by estate, religion, and (increasingly) ethnicity, while in the Soviet Union, people were grouped by class and nationality. Internal passports, vital statistics cards, job applications, and school registration forms relied on these categories to delineate rights and obligations and to shape population policies.[17] Russian rulers did not go to the self-conscious extremes of making race a qualification for membership in communal life, as did Nazi Germany, Jim Crow America, and other racial regimes around the world. But by rejecting the premise that an individual could belong to multiple identities, the state's classification system primed people to see the world in unambiguous racial terms.

Under the old regime, as in Soviet Russia and the turn of the twenty-first century, race-based hatred was rooted in complex and contradictory understandings of racial categories. Scholars who interpret race in crude, biological terms or according to a strict black–white dichotomy, or question its wider impact in the making of social policy tend to ignore its inherent messiness.[18] They also fail to appreciate its subtleties. The power of race lies in its symbolism and invisibility. Although difficult to document historically, it was the subtle aggressions that made race-based hatred such a tremendous burden to bear in the micro-politics of daily life. For the women and men who tried to distance themselves from their ethnic origins—or perhaps looked to pass for another group entirely—the everyday slights, prejudices, dismissals, and verbal abuses, whether conscious or unintentional, served as constant reminders of their true race.[19]

I have no intention of providing a seamless narrative of how race designations grouped and separated populations from one historical era to the next. Drawing on a wide range of historical sources, I raise exploratory questions about the meanings and functions of race. What did racial identifications and categories mean in Russia? What was the relationship between race, whiteness, and geography? How did Russia fit into the global dimensions of the color line? When and why did skin color emerge as an important element in the process of identity formation?

On one level, I explore the ways state actors promoted racial consciousness (the awareness of difference based on religion, customs, and ancestry) and racist attitudes (institutional and popular discriminations based on essential and ultimately unbridgeable differences). This is not to suggest that racialization was inherently a top-down affair, imposed by systems of government at the highest levels, or was dictated by elaborate doctrines or dogmas. To be sure, the rhetoric and policies of government actors—to say nothing of ideologies couched in baseless scientific formulations—played important roles. But I am equally concerned with understanding how ordinary people experienced, struggled with, and negotiated their place in a world where race mattered in surprising and still not entirely understood ways. In what follows, I show that racial categories—and the ideas and practices associated with the production and maintenance of difference—are fundamentally the work of history, shaped by a combination of political, social, ideological, and global forces. It is this troubling story that I tell in the pages that follow.

CHAPTER 1
THE EMPIRE'S RACES

In a sweeping article entitled "On the Goals and Methods of Anthropology," published at the turn of the twentieth century in Russia's leading anthropological journal, Dmitrii Nikolaevich Anuchin marveled at the empire's human diversity. One of Russia's eminent anthropologists, Anuchin taught for more than three decades at Moscow University. He wished to produce an exhaustive map of the empire's races, with the goal of using the most innovative tools the field had to offer to gain a better understanding of the population's racial composition. Such an undertaking would allow experts to make comparisons by considering a wealth of variables, including height and bodily proportions, skin color, hair, eyes, as well as physiological and pathological features that deviated from the statistical norm. In the spirit of cultural pluralism, Anuchin disavowed grand theories of human development, stressing, instead, the role of environmental factors in the creation of racial types.[1]

Racial thinking existed long before the vocabulary of race came into being. The projects and policies of early modern European colonial powers constructed hierarchies and transmitted racial prejudices.[2] But the term "race," as an organizing principle, entered the West European imagination only in the seventeenth century. Scientists and political theorists relied on theories of race to designate populations by common cultural origins and customs, as well as to order humankind according to psychic and physical expressions, bodily features and structures, blood and shared ancestry, and other observable characteristics. European writers used the two terms interchangeably, frequently referring to races as "nations." Although enlightenment thinkers such as the German naturalist theorist Johann Friedrich Blumenbach helped establish a fivefold schema to classify populations (from human types with the most brilliant whiteness of skin to the darkest skin color), many of these ideas were without practical application. The modern, exclusionary forms of racism began to appear across Europe and its colonial world—as a mass phenomenon—in the long nineteenth century. The idea that a hierarchy of humankind could be constructed based on absolute differences formed the essence of modern racism, even if the precise contours varied according to each national context.[3]

The concept of race acquired intellectual prestige in scientific circles. The most respected anthropologists of the day such as Dmitrii Anuchin in Russia or Rudolf Virchow in Germany embraced cultures in all of their diversity. Although both men showed little interest in linking their scholarship to imperialist politics or crude biological thought, they nevertheless believed in the reality of racial thinking: that racial types could be identified by the power of scientific observation. The existence of racial theories—called respectable race science—was deemed to be an important part of social-scientific thought in fin-de-siècle Europe. Scientists, health officials, and journalists relied on racial categories to rank humanity according to established proofs. Some groups such as Jews appropriated the language of race science as a positive form of collective self-expression and self-definition. Even the social scientists who denied the influence of biological determinism on the development of deviance framed their counter arguments in racial terms.[4]

Imperial Russia was no exception to these intellectual developments, although, as with so much else, the debates concerning race emerged later in Russia than they did in Western Europe, North America, and the Atlantic World. The word "*rasa*" appeared in Russia sometime in the second quarter of the nineteenth century. The term acquired two broad meanings that could but did not always overlap.[5] The first, signifying color and following Blumenbach's five varieties, designated races as white, yellow, red, dark, and black. The second, more ambiguous meaning categorized developed groups such as Slavs, Semites, Caucasians, Greco-Romans, and Turko-Tatars, as well as less sophisticated ones such as Poles, Germans, Chinese, Ukrainians, and Jews as "races" (*rasy*), "types" (*tipy*), or "ethnicities" (*narody*)—based on highly elaborate and often contradictory physical features and ethnographic descriptions.

Over the course of the nineteenth century, Russia's social and religious landscape became increasingly fluid. Hoping to make sense of the messiness of empire, statisticians, ethnographers, and anthropologists employed the category of ethnicity (*narodnost'* and *natsional'nost'*) to define difference based on a combination of factors such as language, cultural practices, and religion. While Jews, for instance, could not be distinguished from Germans or Slavs by skin color, they could be identified as "Jews" by ethno-cultural descriptions and anatomical characteristics such as brain size and the shape of the nose. Thus, as ethnicity began to acquire intellectual currency to classify populations, so did the belief that difference was racially fixed—intrinsic, unchangeable, and permanent. The gradual shift in documentation practices—from religion and social estate to ethnicity and race—reflected the changing composition of the empire's population along ethno-cultural lines and did not prove remarkable in the fin de siècle.[6]

Terms were often used interchangeably. Two contemporary dictionaries, *Desk Dictionary for Reference in All Branches of Knowledge* (1864) and *Russian Encyclopedic Dictionary* (1875), defined race as "tribe" (*plemia*). Tribes, in turn, were distinguished by five groupings: (1) white or Indo-European; (2) yellow-skinned or Asiatic; (3) red-skinned or American; (4) dark-skinned; and (5) Black or African. All tribes could be distinguished by specific bodily features such as nose, hair, eyes, and height.[7] The term "*plemia*" referenced specific populations but did not delineate a judgement on their destiny or refer to their status within the empire.[8] The early definition of race or *plemia* established a coherent taxonomy, stressing shared characteristics of humankind.

The Birth of Racism

The Russian field of ethnography was generally characterized by tolerant attitudes toward less developed populations. In their voluminous writings, ethnographers promoted a self-conscious liberal humanism in how they categorized the multiethnic population, paying particular attention to the development of distinct cultural norms and histories.[9] "At no time have we Russians devoted so much time to the study of our fatherland's ethnic groups, as we have in the past ten years," one ethnographer commented in 1872.[10] To be sure, ethnographers, geographers, and administrators referred to *inorodtsy*, or non-Russian peoples of different origins, as "crude," "savage," and "dangerous." Despite these negative assertions, imperial elites had great faith in the civilizing mission: that they could transform the lives of primitive natives by introducing them to Russian ways of life, teaching them the Russian language, and converting them to the dominant Orthodox Russian faith.

Religious toleration provided stability to the imperial state. The Tsars protected the Russian Orthodox Church, as well as all other officially recognized confessions, including Judaism and Islam. Catherine the Great (1729–96) was well aware of both the challenges and limitations of integrating non-Orthodox populations, and especially those peoples residing in the geopolitically sensitive borderland regions. Pragmatic state policies bestowed upon colonial subjects the right to maintain their distinct religious and cultural traditions. Still, the idea of civilizing the unenlightened savage—by introducing the new convert to the Russian way of life and the Christian faith—played an important role in missionary activity. By the beginning of the nineteenth century, large numbers of Russia's non-Christian subjects (somewhere around four million people, many of whom were pagan or Muslim) converted to Orthodoxy. Although sensational cases of intimidation popped up from time to time, coercive proselytizing was not the primary intent of imperial expansion. Instead, government officials offered a wide range of economic benefits, tax incentives, and subsidies for resettlement to increase the attractiveness of conversion.[11]

Conversion turned out to be a slow and burdensome process, even as formal religious transfer offered perquisites to new Christians. The first generation of converts found it challenging to assimilate to their new surroundings; many experienced hostilities from their new communities and their former coreligionists. The imperial government continued to promote Russian Orthodoxy in word and deed. But in the first half of the nineteenth century, some officials began to argue that the regime's missionary zeal needed to be tempered by a healthy skepticism of the convert's motivations. Others voiced reservations about the dangers of forcible conversions. Influential administrators with direct ties to the imperial court expressed skepticism, as well, arguing that all subjects of the empire needed to remain in the confessional church into which they were born.[12]

The idea that religious faith was a matter of birth—and not of personal conviction—had profound implications for the management of the confessional order, as well as for the construction and preservation of group boundaries. The case of Jewish conversion to Christianity provides a striking example of the growing cynicism of baptism. Jews who chose to formally break with their faith found it challenging to distance themselves from family bonds, disown their children, and leave behind the memory of Jewishness. Conversion granted Jews the legal right to start a new life beyond the Pale of Settlement (where most Jews lived, with some exceptions, until the collapse of the imperial order). But somewhere in the mid-nineteenth century, officials began to sound the alarm. Long after their religious transfer, baptized Jews continued to be seen as belonging to the "Jewish race." The imperial Russian government, responding to the challenges of maintaining clear distinctions, decided to erect barriers. In 1850, the State Council mandated that all converts retain their surnames (upon baptism Jews were ordered to adopt new forenames and patronymics), reasoning that a Jewish-sounding last name would increase the visibility of the new convert and hinder total integration. Imperial administrators' skepticism of the transformative power of Christian rites grew in the last years of the old regime. As racial thinking became widespread, so did the stigma associated with Jewishness (a theme I will discuss in greater detail in Chapter 2).[13]

Skulls, Brains, and the Race Question

In the second half of the nineteenth century, two important developments helped to construct increasingly impermeable boundaries. First, in Russia as in other European countries, the disciplines of physical anthropology, criminology, and medicine relied on tools of social knowledge based on statistics, quantitative measurements, and visual representations. The turn from a textual tradition—the province of ethnographic work—to what was regarded as an objective methodology premised on the power of numbers and visuals signified an important innovation in the social-scientific gaze. Anthropologists amassed impressive mounds of data to substantiate their claims. They employed the technique of anthropometry to measure and rank bodily features such as skulls, widely considered the primordial racial trait, directly linked to brain size. They turned to photography to illustrate arguments based on scrutinizable body parts, as well as the invisible or hard-to-read differences.[14]

In a review essay of physical anthropology in Russia and the West, Anuchin explained why the discipline began to garner respect for technological innovations in the analysis of skulls, brains, and other bodily features: "There is no doubt that in the near future the importance of anthropology will be even more widespread, that in time it will take a visible place in the field of scientific inquiry. Biologists, doctors, historians, philosophers, and even ordinary educated persons will realize the importance of a greater scientific 'knowledge of oneself.'"[15] Statistical measurements made it easier to compare anatomical peculiarities among racial groups, establishing common perceptions of deviance and pathology.

Second, the trust in numerical representation provided scientific credibility to common stereotypes and observations. Poles, Jews, Chinese, and other yellow races were perceived as some of the most loathed groups in the empire, subject to discriminatory legislation, but nearly all race scientists agreed that only the Jews represented a unified racial type.[16] Ideologies of anti-Jewish hatred expressed the fears and anxieties of the age. A popular textbook published at the turn of the twentieth century described Jews in the following manner: "In all other countries, the primeval Jew has nearly disappeared, acquiring the manners and customs of the peoples around him. In Russia, on the contrary, [the Jew] has retained his type and ways of life." Written in an easy to comprehend manner, with the mission of educating the general public about the empire's ethnic diversity, the authors emphasized the Jew's distinctiveness: "This is a person from another part of the world, of another race, in physical, as well as moral, dimensions."[17]

Anthropometric measurements and photographic representations of racial types revealed curious patterns of behavior, helping construct a powerful image of difference, while enshrining deterministic hierarchies. Although a familiar phrase, modernist race science repackaged the conception into a series of discourses predicated on positivist science. Jews' bodies, for example, were described as weak, unhealthy, and unfit for performing social duties such as military service. The descriptions acquired credibility because the very essence of human frailty – chest sizes, muscular strength, and physical incapacity – could be objectively measured and compared to "fitter" races. Anthropometric measurements helped substantiate the claim that Jews possessed smaller chests and other physical peculiarities in comparison to other racial groups.[18] In Russia, as in Germany and Austria-Hungary, journalists and administrators argued routinely that narrow chest sizes and height prevented Jews from fulfilling military obligations and becoming productive soldiers.[19]

The social thinkers who came of age in the 1860s and 1870s—whether liberal, conservative, or Populist—embraced Darwin's principle of natural selection but rejected the Social Darwinist understanding of individualistic competition and conflict, viewing the progressive development among species and humankind in terms of mutual cooperation. To quote the famous anarchist and social thinker Petr Kropotkin, "We [Russians] see a great deal of mutual aid where Darwin and Wallace see only struggle."[20] One of the broader implications of this line of reasoning resulted in the valorization of environmentalism: that social conditions and not biology shaped relations among humankind, the development of normalcy, and the evolution of physical characteristics.[21]

The language of race had great appeal for Russia's scientists. Hardly any expert who kept up with the latest scholarly findings denied the existence of racial categories, even if they questioned the role that biology played in the construction of differences. In the Russian Empire, as in Central Europe and the Atlantic World, medical language about how each race experienced disease grew out of a constellation of ideas in circulation at the time.[22] Following the lead of their German-Jewish counterparts, Jewish social scientists, for instance, relied on the power of numbers to construct a powerful counter narrative to the racially deterministic model. "The majority of [medical] experts consider Jews the most nervous people in the world," an entry read in the *Jewish Encyclopedia* on nervous and psychological illnesses.[23] Jewish social scientists, hoping to revise theories of Jewish essentialism, came to the conclusion that the Jewish race, always shaped by environmental factors, was prone to hysteria, neurasthenia, and epilepsy, among other medical disorders.

What made Jews so susceptible to the disorders? Experts put forward a broad spectrum of sociological explanations—from climate and economy to culture and hygiene—which contributed to the racial peculiarities. Parents forced children to study in dark and unhygienic primary schools, causing children to develop degenerate states of mind, while prolonged exposure to social and economic isolation played no small role in fostering the abnormalities.[24] Significantly, Jewish social scientists did not disagree with the statistical evidence, but they nevertheless came up with their own explanations for the apparent differences. It turned out that the distancing from biological laws of development did not isolate the Russian scientific community from the worldwide debates concerning nature and nurture. Russian social scientists shared their skepticism about the determinism of heredity with many of their colleagues abroad. Stressing the importance of the forces of evolution, or neo-Lamarckism, they believed in the ability of all races to progress.[25]

In Russia, as in Europe and North America, physical anthropology emerged as a respected academic discipline in the last decades of the nineteenth century. The ethnographic division of the Russian Geographical Society – as well as Moscow University's Society of Admirers of Natural Science, Ethnography, and Anthropology (founded in 1863) and Kazan University's Society of Archaeology, History, and Ethnography (founded in 1878) – served as important predecessors to the rise of the anthropological profession. One of the founders of Russian anthropology, Anatolii Petrovich Bogdanov was influenced by none other than Paul Broca, the ambitious polygenist professor of anatomy at the Faculté de Médecine in Paris. Bogdanov took craniometrical measurements of skulls, which he personally excavated from Moscow cemeteries, to demonstrate the biological reality of racial types. He organized a highly successful exhibition that displayed many of Russia's anthropological, archaeological, and ethnographic collections in Moscow University's Museum of Anthropology.[26]

Over the years, Bogdanov also helped train some of the most brilliant anthropologists, including Anuchin, who played a formative role in establishing the Moscow school of physical anthropology. Both men read widely in the international theoretical literature on race and human development, participated in conferences and workshops in Europe, and played no small role in establishing anthropology as a distinct profession with an international reputation. The Department of Anthropology was first established in 1876 at Moscow University. The Ministry of Education refused to include the discipline of anthropology in the 1884 university statute and, instead, created a department of geography. As a newly appointed professor of geography, Anuchin did not let institutional politics deter him from his intellectual commitments. Anuchin continued the work that he had begun under Bogdanov's supervision: conducting anthropological research and reading lectures on physical anthropology, the history of anthropology, the origins of man, and ethnology.[27]

In contrast to German anthropology's provincial worldliness, Russian anthropology was marked by an imperial regionalism – the preoccupation with the vast territories, peoples, and cultures of the empire.[28] Some of the most influential studies were published in Moscow University's *Russkii antropologicheskii zhurnal* (Russian Anthropological Journal, founded in 1900). Dissertations on non-Russian peoples were written at the St. Petersburg Military Medical Academy. Although St. Petersburg and Moscow played important roles in scientific research, Russian anthropologists were deeply attentive to conducting research across the vast spaces of the empire. The fascination with local cultures provided the impetus to establish ethnographic and archaeological museums in the provinces. Kazan, Kharkov, and Kiev emerged as important centers for production of anthropological research. Designed to display the empire's regional identities, museums popped up in places such as Novgorod, Vladimir, Samara, Astrakhan, Vladikavkaz, Kherson, Ekaterinoslav, and Minsk.

For the anthropologists, the empire's unparalleled diversity consumed and at the same time complicated the work. "The ethnic composition of Russia's population is distinguished by an astonishing physical as well as cultural diversity," the anthropologist Aleksei Arsen'evich Ivanovskii wrote in a review article of *inorodtsy*, "which we do not find in any West European country." "All the ethnic groups and all the tribes develop their own particular racial characteristics [*razlichnye chelovecheskie rasy*]," he argued.[29] The physical traits, Ivanovskii insisted, could be distinguished by skin color, the shape of the head, and the distinctiveness of the face.

Jewish Exceptionalism?

Russian anthropology's concern with non-Russians – their experiences, cultures, and physical characteristics – shaped the scientific program. The territories of the empire and its diverse populations constituted one of the world's richest laboratories for anthropological investigations. "In these vast territories reside many physical types, with diverse lifestyles and different stages of cultural development," Anuchin wrote. "Comparative anthropological analysis should help explain the racial composition of the populations, establish their types, and allow the researcher to make comparisons with similar peoples of the world."[30] Anuchin lamented, however, that Russian anthropologists could not make the kinds of empirical comparisons that their German and French counterparts were able to make. Whereas their colleagues abroad made comparisons based on "objective," or numerical, indices, Russia's anthropologists relied mostly on descriptive observations originally compiled by ethnographers and linguists. "Regardless of our achievements," Ivanovskii wrote in 1902, "the anthropological profession finds itself in a preparatory stage; the collection of materials is far from adequate for making a systematic classification of the empire's multiethnic population."[31]

In spite of the inadequacies, Ivanovskii proceeded to create a classificatory map of Russia's racial groups. Although much raw statistical data had been collected, the materials had not been collectively ordered, processed, or analyzed. "Without a doubt," Ivanovskii began his study entitled "An Attempt at the Classification of the Population of Russia," "one of the most significant impediments to the development of Russian anthropology is the absence of systematized, collected data." Ivanovskii wanted to create a preliminary typology based on ten indices that could be easily measured and compared: (1) color of hair and eyes, (2) height, (3) size of head, (4) cranial measurements, (5) absolute length of face, (6) nose, (7) size of torso, (8) width of chest, (9) size of arms, (10) size of legs.[32]

Ivanovskii hoped to isolate the racial characteristics that would allow him to compare populations. To his surprise, he found it difficult to distinguish one ethnic group from another based on a particular physical trait or racial purity. Based on a wealth of scientific measurements, he concluded that the indices did not isolate the empire's populations but blended them together. Belarusians, for example, could not be easily distinguished from Ukrainians or Poles, Azerbaijani Tatars from Kurds, or Kalmyks from Iakuts. But he did find one exception: the Jews. Jews confounded anthropological thinking. "On the whole," he wrote, "Jews form a complete and an entirely isolated anthropological type not joined to any other [racial] group." Even if the claim was based on a small sample, Ivanovskii conceded, the data suggested that Jews formed a distinct race. By the color of the hair and eyes, the Jew constituted a dark racial type; by the size of the body, the Jew was deemed unusually small; and by the length of the chest, the Jew was viewed as sickly, weak, and underdeveloped. Cranial measurements – the gold standard in rigorous quantitative analysis – revealed that a statistically significant number of Jews were brachycephalic (or round-headed), a trait usually equated with primitive European inhabitants rather than the more progressive dolichocephalic (or long-headed) peoples.[33]

Numerous other studies confirmed that Jews constituted a unique, biologically pure race. The anthropologist A. D. El'kind observed that, "regardless of the geographic territory in which they reside, Jews can be more or less distinguished by their anthropometric and physiognomic characteristics."[34] The most unique physical characteristic of the Jews was the brain. In a highly detailed comparative study, the anthropologist R. L. Vainberg showed that "Jews belong to those peoples with comparatively small brains" that do not conform to either "normal" or "typical" human brains. The structural composition of the Jewish brain was closer to that of the less developed peoples (as opposed, for instance, to Slavs who possessed larger-sized brains). The Jewish brain, moreover, weighed less than that of the more civilized peoples.[35] In his dissertation on the Jews of Mogilev province, written at the Military Medical Academy, Mikhail Georgievich Iakovenko made a similar observation regarding the biological purity of Jews. Iakovenko demonstrated that Jews could be easily distinguished by their nose (specifically their nostrils, which were categorized as type two nostrility due to the irregular extensions of the nostril passages that divided sharply at the tip of the nose).[36]

The language of race science made its appearance in Russia toward the end of the nineteenth century. Russia's scientific experts, journalists, and medical doctors read, reviewed, and critiqued the literature in academic journals and mass circulation periodicals. They engaged in heated discussions concerning the role that environmental or biological factors (and sometimes a strange mixture of the two) played in producing physiological peculiarities, social deviance and pathology, and criminal behavior. While participating in the discussions, Russia's race scientists usually distanced themselves from crude biological thought. Acknowledging the limits of social-scientific research, they called for more data to comprehend the role that environment, intermarriage, and biology, among many other factors, played in the construction of racial types – reservations they shared with other race scientists in England, Germany, and France, where intense debates ensued over the efficacy of race as an explanatory category.[37]

Although Russia's scientific community did not add a qualitative dimension to their arguments, it did not take long for mass consumer culture to repackage a highly academic discourse to the public. Ideas, however, are not self-contained entities. They take on new forms and functions as they are transmitted into people's minds.[38] How were beliefs in human differences expressed in the subjective dimensions of social relations? What role did visual imagery play in stirring up racist thought and behavior? How did stereotypes, common perceptions, and visual representations affirm collective prejudices? It is to an examination of these questions – or how ideas in fixed or absolute differences played out in policy, behavior, and daily life – that we now turn.

CHAPTER 2
BOUNDARIES OF EXCLUSION

What was the most straightforward way of distinguishing a Pole from a Russian or a Russian from a Jew? Imperial authorities, in their efforts to maintain clear distinctions between populations, were particularly interested in preserving order and stability. Since Russia's westward expansion in the eighteenth century, administrators viewed the western borderlands with a deep sense of weakness and suspicion. During the reign of Tsar Alexander II (1855–81), paternalist thinking resulted in a host of measures designed to protect Russian peasants from the more resourceful Germans, Poles, and Jews. To expedite adaptation to Russian norms and language, Alexander II adopted a policy of gradual administrative and cultural Russification. Although the most zealous Russifiers could not agree on the exact terms, they usually pointed out that the essence of Russianness had something to do with language and religion and that Russification was a gradual process, taking one or more generations to complete. One of the most pressing concerns was the establishment of Russian as the official language in bureaucracy and schools. Other areas of reform included elevating the dominant position of the Orthodox Church vis-à-vis other Christian confessions, while bringing municipal and judicial institutions into a greater degree of conformity with those of European Russia.[1]

Following the assassination of his father, on March 1, 1881, Tsar Alexander III (1881–94) sought to work out a new political model for Russian autocratic rule. The political conservatism of Alexander III's reign marked the appearance of an exclusionary imperial racism in all walks of political life. As a deep pessimism gripped the empire, Alexander III and his advisers decided to dig deeper than their predecessors. The disorders following the assassination of Tsar Alexander II, including outbreaks of anti-Jewish violence in the southwestern borderlands, offered the new emperor the occasion to repudiate the gradualism of the previous reign. To embolden the principle of ethnic supremacy of the Russian majority, Alexander III subjugated non-Russian populations to forceful Russification practices, bolstered the powers of the police, and implemented measures to identify and segregate populations by ethno-racial markers.[2]

The Jewish Problem

In the western borderlands, ethnic minorities, including Poles and, to a lesser extent, Ukrainians, suffered as a consequence of the state's reactionary policies, but it was the Jewish problem that took center stage. Much like perceptions of Blacks in the United States and in European colonial empires, anti-Jewish images became a universal feature of governmental policy and public opinion: Jews, it was reasoned, threatened to undermine, perhaps even destroy, the social order from within.

Public opinion lamented that the Jewish race possessed characteristics which would not allow them to assimilate. "What the Jews were, so they shall remain," the conservative *Novoe vremia* (The New Times) opined. Even the liberal *Golos* (The Voice) felt that "the Semitic race, for all its aptitudes, possesses many qualities which make it far from a sympathetic object for [ethnic] Russians."[3] Some of the fears corresponded to the general paranoia that crossed international borders; others were grounded in the realities of imperial Russian history (by the remarkable participation of Jews in radical and revolutionary movements). That the majority of the political criminals came from the empire's western borderlands and that a high percentage of all those sentenced happened to be Jewish only reinforced the fears that Jews threatened the prosperity and tranquility of the empire.[4]

By the last decades of the nineteenth century, Jews constituted an unmistakable presence in public life and were drawn to some of the fastest growing cities in the empire, including Kiev, Odessa, St. Petersburg, and Moscow. Jews were overly represented in gymnasia and universities, in law and medicine, and in music schools and the visual arts. They dominated commercial life, tax-farming, small-scale trade, manufacturing industries, sugar mills, and gold mines.[5] Partly as a response to the growing visibility of Jews, public opinion accepted the pernicious claim that Jews posed a direct economic threat to Russian society. According to minister of interior Count Nikolai Pavlovich Ignatiev, the most urgent duty of the government was to take measures to "safeguard" the native population from the harmful activity of the Jews.

Ignatiev served as the chief architect of temporary legislative measures known as the May Laws, ratified on May 3, 1882. By forbidding Jewish residence outside urban settlements and carrying on trade on Sundays and the twelve major feasts of the Orthodox Church, the May Laws attempted to draw a distinct line between Jews and their Christian neighbors. With nearly 600,000 individuals targeted for expulsion, Jews became objects of frequent roundups, abuse, and police surveillance.[6] Segregationist policies did not create an absolute divide between Jews and peasants or towns and villages. But together with the quota system, designed to limit the number of Jews in institutions of public education and the free professions, discussed in more detail later, the state's expulsion policies made life frustratingly difficult for Jewish communities.

Imperial law placed undue burdens on Jewish mobility. A mosaic of complex statutes prohibited Jews from residing in places except those that were delineated in the law codes. Initially, the Pale of Settlement was designed not to segregate Jews, but to confine Jews to the fifteen western provinces. The idea was to contain Jews in a region where they had lived prior to the partitions of the Polish–Lithuanian Commonwealth.[7] But during the Great Reform era, as Russia underwent remarkable economic growth, and as certain groups such as merchants of the first and second guild, students in institutions of higher education, and select artisans received the right to reside in the heartland of the empire, the laws associated with the delineation of the Pale of Settlement came to symbolize the most repressive of Tsarist policies.

In the 1870s and 1880s, the passport statutes proved especially onerous for Jewish daily life. One journalist remarked, in 1877, that no other European capital had such harsh laws that constrained where Jews could live and how long they could travel. "Upon birth a Jew is deprived of the freedom to move and the right to choose a place of residence—the most basic of all individual and civil rights—rights which all other subjects of the empire enjoy, with the exception of Jews."[8] In St. Petersburg, Moscow, and Kiev, authorities carried out sweeps of neighborhoods in search of illegal migrants, expelling Jews for not practicing the occupation listed in their residence papers or for acquiring a fictitious social identity. Over the years, Jews endured numerous financial hardships and lasting psychological damage as a consequence of the state's passport laws. Reactionary newspapers spread mass hysteria by publishing accounts of Jews violating passport laws and refusing to return to their permanent place of residence. Expulsions caused unprecedented fear and violence, but they did not resemble mass ethnic cleansing practices, or the total removal of a population by ethnic criteria. The Russian government had no intention of keeping Jews in one place—of making the Pale of Settlement an ethnically pure space.

Just as the concept of the racially fixed Jew started to acquire popular resonance, the boundaries between Jews and everyone else became increasingly difficult to police. By changing names, mores, and religion, Jews were able to erase or in some cases conceal some of the most prominent symbols of their identities, making it difficult to know who was Jewish and where Jews were. The illegibility of Jews did not go unnoticed. The search for a dependable indicator of Jewishness led in different directions. Religion and language no longer served as dependable markers of identity. In the spirit of elevating Russianness, bureaucrats came up with creative ways to mark Jews as a distinctive population. In St. Petersburg, Moscow, and Warsaw, police officials required Jewish merchants to display forenames, patronymics, and surnames on all privately owned shops. The Ministry of the Interior and the Holy Synod spent considerable energy compiling an exhaustive book of "Jewish" names—to help determine who exactly was Jewish by making sure that Yiddish diminutives, Hebrew biblical, and Russian names were spelled correctly in vital statistic books, censuses, and passports.[9]

Conservative critics, in the 1870s and beyond, painted a dark picture of the visibility of Jews and other ethnic minorities in institutions of higher education. A highly influential letter to the editor of *Novoe vremia* entitled "The Kike is Coming!" warned that Jews were on the verge of dominating "not only [commercial and financial] professions, but also the so-called liberal professions," allowing them to command immense material and intellectual power.[10] The public debate over the number of Jews in higher education intensified after the pogroms of 1881 and 1882 and the student unrest of the 1880s. Both Jews and other ethnic minorities such as Poles were subjected to ethnically based quotas, mostly due to fears that they would take away jobs from ethnic Russians. State-sanctioned quotas limited Jewish access to public gymnasia, technical schools, and universities. At Russia's eight universities, the quota of Jewish students ranged from 3 percent in St. Petersburg and 4 percent in Moscow to 24 percent in Odessa and 27 percent in Kharkov. Private schools and academies occasionally followed suit. In Kiev, the Volodkevich Women's Commercial School capped the number of Jewish students, while one local gymnasium forbade Jewish students from tutoring its Christian students. Quotas were also introduced for non-Russians in cadet schools, but only the Jews were banned outright.[11]

Despite the efforts to draw social boundaries, large metropolises, as well as many smaller provincial settlements and market towns, offered an eclectic mix of people, including Russian Orthodox peasants, German colonists, Jews, Poles, and Ukrainians, among others, opportunities to socialize at marketplaces, at street fairs, and in neighborhood taverns. As part of Russia's emerging civil society, voluntary organizations—charities, libraries, and cultural clubs—provided common space for people from different backgrounds to mix, forge partnerships, and cooperate on some level.

The few Black Americans who lived and worked in imperial Russia commented that they could pursue whatever likelihoods they chose. Frederick Bruce Thompson—also known as Fyodor Fyodorovich Tomas—grew up in the Deep South in the Reconstruction Era. His travels took him to Chicago, New York, and across the Atlantic to England and France. Eventually, Frederick entered Russia and rose to prominence in Moscow's theater world. Before the cataclysmic events of 1917 toppled the old order, Frederick owned two of Moscow's celebrated nightclubs, making millions in today's money. His mixed-race children attended one of the elite schools in the country. For Frederick, as for Russia's tiny colony of Black residents, race did not appear to be an issue.[12]

Yet, for certain despised groups a noticeable shift occurred in the ways in which hierarchies were drawn and inequalities were justified. Following the abortive Polish rebellion of 1863, officials became increasingly fearful of Catholicism and of Poles spreading harmful ideas in Russian institutions. More than 300 Catholic churches, chapels, and monasteries were shuttered. Over 300,000 Catholics were forcibly converted to Russian Orthodoxy. The regime relocated thousands of Poles from the western borderlands to Siberia. It also restored strict censorship laws, suppressed the nascent revolutionary movement, and issued new regulations to staff bureaucracies with "true Russians." M. N. Murav'ev, the governor-general of the northwest provinces, came up with bold schemes to exclude "persons of Polish origins" from civil service or teaching jobs and to cleanse the region of Poles. Alexander II did his part by ratifying restrictive decrees forbidding Polish Catholics from working as teachers in educational institutions controlled by the Ministry of Enlightenment. To combat unwelcome Polish influences, Murav'ev proposed to cap the number of students of Polish origins at no more than 10 percent.[13]

Associational life brought people together, but laws limited where Poles and especially Jews could live, work, study, and socialize. Despite the integrationist currents, Western travelers noticed that Jews were often called the Negroes of Russia. Voluntary organizations played on societal fears, segregating populations by religion and, increasingly, ethno-racial origins (*proiskhozhdenie*). Both Jews and baptized Jews were targeted disproportionately for abuse. The restrictive laws multiplied at the turn of the twentieth century. The Congress of the United Nobility insisted on excluding Jews and Jewish converts from serving in the army, navy, and all military schools. The Union of Agrarians denied membership to Jews and baptized Jews. Municipal libraries in Berdichev and Bobruisk (where a large majority of the population was Jewish) refused to subscribe to Jewish books and periodicals. In Kiev, populist politicians promoted legislation to limit Jewish economic opportunities, while some high-ranking administrators insisted that certain institutions such as hospitals and schools should serve only the city's Christian population.[14]

Conversion to Christianity lifted the formal restrictions associated with Jewishness. But as racial thinking became more pronounced and as hostilities to Jews increased, baptized Jews experienced prejudice in their daily lives. The individuals who opted to formally change their religion to Russian Orthodoxy, Catholicism, or Protestantism usually did so for strategic reasons: to receive residential privileges beyond the Pale of Settlement in cities such as Moscow or St. Petersburg, to get around official quotas in institutions of higher education, to work in the profession of their choice, or to marry a Christian spouse. Some individuals experienced difficulties in removing the signs and symbols associated with their Jewish past. Others encountered bureaucratic discrimination in public life. It did not help matters that authorities were continually preoccupied with maintaining distinctions between new converts and "real" Christians, including marking *iz evreev* (of Jewish origins) on official documents for Russian Orthodox converts.[15]

Ultimately, the deep cultural pessimism that gripped Russia in the fin de siècle had far-reaching consequences on day-to-day encounters. Burdened by slights, slurs, and rejections, baptized Jews found it difficult to hide their background in both their private and public lives.[16] For Pavel Osipovich Eizenberg, a Russian Orthodox convert, the descriptor "of Jewish origins" in his passport not only offended his sensibilities, but it also meant that he could not easily pass as Russian.[17] Sofiia Silberman, who had converted to Russian Orthodoxy to marry her Christian lover, petitioned for a similar reason: this time, to change the Jewish surnames of her children so they would not endure insulting questions in their adult lives. In the petition, she wrote that her children "suffer from ridicule and questions from their peers for carrying a Jewish surname, 'Zilberman.'" "Why," she asked, "should she suffer for sins she did not commit and constantly feel the backhanded glances of those around her?"[18] The process of reinvention—of erasing the stigmas and symbols of Jewishness—proved difficult to overcome.

The 1905 Revolution served as a major turning point in the intensification of racial prejudice. On January 9, 1905, troops set off months of revolutionary protests by shooting on a demonstration of unarmed workers. In the aftermath of Bloody Sunday, the civil order broke down. Russia experienced a massive assault on its authority, including a wave of politically motivated strikes. Adopting exclusionary language and violent means, right-wing populists argued that Russia's institutions existed solely to support "true Russians." Right-wing extremist groups benefited from the relaxed laws on voluntary associations, publishing, and expression. Militant nationalists founded clubs and organizations. They staged public protests, festivals, and rallies. Some published their own newspapers and brochures, which they used to widen their reach by peddling conspiracy theories.

In moments of crisis, right-wing organizations such as the Monarchist Russian Society, a precursor to the paramilitary organization, Black Hundreds, exhorted ethnic Russians to defend their people and territory, at the expense of Jews and other ethnic minorities:

> Beat the damned traitors everywhere and all over, wherever you find them and with whatever [you can], beat the Yids, destroyers of the Russian tsardom, beat the bloodthirsty robbers in the zemstvo [local governments], beat the instigators of the sedition and strikes, beat . . . the school youth, even if he would be your son, brother, or relative, all the same he's a traitor, don't pity [him], beat him, he's a complete wretch and is the destroyer of the people and the Russian land, the more of them we destroy, the better for Russia and [for] the people, the more of them we kill, the less sedition there will be in Russia and Russia will be on the path of redemption.[19]

The right-wing movement—with more than 300,000 active members—thrived in cities and towns with sizeable Jewish populations. Diverse in their ideological stance and social profile, paramilitary groups received protection from powerful local officials. The Black Hundreds threatened and occasionally unleashed violence

Image 2.1 Postcard featuring the Union of the Russian People, the most popular of the organizations promoting extreme-right ideologies. Founded in 1905, the organization was known for its anti-Semitic and Russocentric doctrines and strong support of the autocracy. © Courtesy of Popperfoto via Getty Images.

on Jewish communities in Odessa and Kishinev. In Kiev, anti-liberal populists described pogroms as an act of resistance by people aligned with "truly Russian" interests against Jewish economic exploitation and revolutionary subversion.[20] The Union of the Russian People, the largest, most influential right-wing organization in the empire with more than 800 branches in existence in 1907, acquired a broad following by skillfully manipulating mass media. The organization disseminated thousands of flyers; its main newspaper, *Russkoe znamia* (The Russian Banner), had a daily circulation of between 12,000 and 15,000 copies.[21]

It is well known that Nicholas II (1894–1917) cozied up to right-wing extremists, but newly discovered archival evidence suggests that some of these groups received support through secret channels from the highest reaches of the bureaucracy, including the Ministries of Finance and Interior, to subsidize publishing efforts, organize congresses, and purchase guns. One of the most prominent associations, the Kiev Club of Russian Nationalists, with some 600 members, expanded its base by drawing on long-standing tropes of Polish and Jewish exploitation. At one of the club's events, Ivan A. Sikorskii, a professor of psychiatry at St. Vladimir University, described the ongoing tensions in the borderlands as a racial war between Jews and Poles against the "Aryan" East Slavs.[22]

The uptick in anti-Jewish violence and microaggressions occurred in the midst of explosive labor unrest and of rising concern about crime. If in 1904 there were sixty-eight strikes in which less than 25,000 workers took part, a year later, the numbers surged to nearly 14,000 with more than 2.86 million participants.[23] Many sectors experienced profound politicization. The mass circulation press expanded dramatically in this period, from 123 newspapers in 1898 to more than 1,150 in 1913 and from some 1,000 magazines and journals in 1900 to over 3,000 in 1914.[24] Commentators, on all sides of the political spectrum, characterized the age in exceptionally bleak terms.[25] At the height of revolutionary fervor, newspapers were filled with all sorts of crime stories, from petty theft, mugging, prostitution, and domestic violence to organized crime run by powerful, well-connected rings. Odessa gained a reputation as the empire's criminal capital, although the intensity of the urban violence was on display in many other settings, as well. What started out as mass fistfights could easily evolve into massive public brawls and riots, involving thousands of people (as it did in St. Petersburg), resulting in extensive damage to entire neighborhoods, including shops, theaters, parks, and restaurants.[26]

The brutality of anti-Jewish violence easily surpassed that of earlier incidents. Over the course of two years, in 1905 and 1906, nearly 660 pogroms broke out in the Pale of Settlement, resulting in more than 3,100 Jewish deaths and a colossal 57 million rubles of damage to Jewish property. The populations that deemed themselves as superior applied force on the basis of group membership. Rioters expressed pent-up emotions by blaming Jews for societal ills. Although the violence against Jews was not engineered from above by high-ranking officials, it is hard to absolve provincial authorities from responsibility. In Odessa and many other sites of anti-Jewish violence, pogromist agitators spread wild rumors of Jews fomenting social disorders and slaughtering Christian residents with abandon. Local officials, for their part, often failed to adopt adequate countermeasures, suppress false rumors and propaganda, and contain popular rage from spiraling out of control.[27]

The figure of the Jew was featured prominently in Russian popular culture. Reactionary journalists, politicians, and paramilitary organizations, including the Black Hundreds, circulated images of Jews – with thick lips, oversized eyes, hooked noses, and long, dark hair—sucking the blood of mother Russia, plotting an international conspiracy of domination. Numerous ideologically tainted discourses, including the language of race science, helped define the Jewish problem. Satirical journals, lowbrow magazines, journalism, and postcards all published cartoons that portrayed Jews with stereotypical features. The images showcased were crude, commonplace, and not all that remarkable in and of themselves. Similar unflattering depictions of Jews circulated throughout Europe and across the Atlantic. Their importance lay largely in the symbolic and emotional realms—by providing the public a script: that the Jew was the chief source of Russia's problems.[28]

The Yellow Peril

On the opposite end of the empire, in the far-eastern zone—an expansive, sparsely populated territory of more than 1,200,000 square miles bordering northeast China—the population that sparked similar apprehensions was the East Asians or "yellows," as they were wont to be called.[29] The commonalities between anti-Jewish thinking and anti-Asian prejudice were many, as journalists, business leaders, and Tsarist officials remarked in public forums. Fears of occupation, economic dominance and entrapment, legal controls, and demographic decline all provoked everyday violence and discrimination in both the far-western borderlands (toward Jews and Poles) and the far-eastern periphery (toward Chinese, Koreans, and Japanese).[30] Accusations of exploitation—the buying and reselling of goods at excessive profit—followed a similar pattern for both Chinese and Jewish traders and entrepreneurs. "The Chinese," a journalist writing for the *Sibirskii vestnik* (The Siberian Herald) noted, "are playing a similar role on our eastern frontier as the Jews in our western borderlands, with all of the same consequences."[31]

By 1860, Russia extended its influence in the Far East, establishing the Amur and Ussuri rivers as the new border with China. Eastward expansion created new opportunities for cultural contacts between Russia's subjects and Asiatic peoples. Between 1885 and 1913, around five million subjects crossed the Urals to settle in Asiatic Russia. Local officials and statisticians usually categorized this population—comprised of ethnic Russians, Ukrainians, Latvians, Germans, and a handful of Jews—simply as "Russians." They came to colonize sparsely inhabited land, to trade goods and merchandise, and to participate in large-scale mining and railway construction projects.[32]

Along the far-eastern border, Russian officials perceived Chinese and Korean labor migrants as a distinct threat to the geopolitical stability of the state and the development of its economic interests, even as an unusually high percentage of foreigners were hired for their low cost of labor. In the mid-1880s, the Chinese constituted approximately a third of the population in the Amur and the Ussuri regions. Some were nomadic peoples of mixed Chinese-Manchu origin. The vast majority (mostly men) were skilled and unskilled day laborers. By the first decade of the twentieth century, as many as 550,000 Chinese entered the Russian Empire, while tens of thousands of Koreans traveled back and forth across the far-eastern border. Most East Asian migrants came to work in the gold mines, timber, railroad construction, petty trade, and fishing.[33]

The arrival of Chinese laborers followed similar patterns to those of the United States and the British colony of Victoria. In their attempts to regulate the flow of populations, Russian officials were guided, in large part, by California's policies on Chinese immigration. In the 1880s, America's race prejudices portrayed the Chinese as distinct threats to the health and prosperity of the nation. As a result, thousands of Chinese labor migrants in America were singled out for exclusion based on race. The violence that followed reconfigured American gatekeeping and dramatically expanded the surveillance of the United States border.[34] The Russian government took notice. Over the years, Russia experimented with an assortment of border control methods—from taxes and permits to passports and population quotas. As in America and other places around the world, the efforts to control the border were fueled by sensational media depictions of cunning, dirty, and deceitful Asian migrants.[35]

Large numbers of Chinese and Korean migrants crossed the expansive far-eastern border. On the Russian side of the border, it did not take long for the Chinese to establish a complex of shops, restaurants, and small businesses, including entire quarters, helping fuel a rapidly expanding labor market. Border towns—from Khabarovsk and Vladivostok to Nikolsk, Blagoveshchensk, and Chita—were populated by Chinese farmers, merchants, peddlers, tradesmen, and seasonal laborers. The Chinese dominated gold mines, shipyards, and the railway. They managed most shops and river piers; provided a market for furs, ginseng, antlers, grain, fruits, dry goods, and vegetables; transported contraband and exotic powders across state lines, including opium; and performed essential unskilled labor. At the turn of the twentieth century, census takers determined that eight out of ten diggers were Chinese, as were nine out of ten workers in the shipyards and nearly all the laborers on the Ussuri Line, the Chinese Eastern Railroad, and the Amur Line.[36]

Image 2.2 A photograph of Chinese railway workers eating lunch. At the turn of the twentieth century, the Chinese had become a vital presence on the Russian side of the border. © Public Domain, Wikimedia Commons.

Chita, the capital of the Transbaikal, was one of the most developed cities in Siberia, with a population of approximately 50,000 people. It served as an important junction of the Trans-Siberian Railroad, with a direct trunk line to the Chinese border. With thousands of workers traveling back and forth across the border each year, Chita developed into one of the most vibrant transportation hubs in the region. The visibility of the yellow race did not go unnoticed. Chinese shops and stands on street corners were a common sight in the city. One provincial newspaper observed that the "Chinese have flooded the entire Amur border and are heading further and further [in land]. In Chita, Japanese laundry mats and photography studios have surfaced; [and] the Chinese have taken over digging in the gold mines."[37]

The construction of the Chinese Eastern Railroad—a project that helped establish Russia's colonial sphere of influence in Manchuria –

stimulated economic development by making trade faster and cheaper from the Baltic Sea to the Pacific Ocean. To promote economic interests, Russia abolished, temporarily, the principle of free trade in the territories east of Lake Baikal. Customs posts popped up, but it was nearly impossible to control cross-border movement or to stop the illicit transfer of commodities. Silk, tobacco, and liquor were among the most popular contraband items. Gold, in particular, smuggled from Russia to China by train, horseback, or on a boat, involved a complex network of smugglers, diggers, and traffickers with ties to world markets.[38]

Russian officials attempted to control the Sino-Russian border by stationing patrol agents and instituting customs points and passport requirements. Predictably, the eastern border proved challenging to police. Chinese migrants traveled back and forth, with the pace of migration increasing exponentially with the building of the Chinese Eastern Railroad. Russian customs officials and border patrol agents tried to expel unregistered workers, but experienced guides procured counterfeit passports and circumvented check points. The physical descriptions on the passports—"black hair," "brown eyes," and "short stature"—described most East Asian border crossers.[39]

Chinese and Koreans incited racist fears, not least because of their numbers. S. M. Dukhovskoi, appointed as the Amur governor-general in 1893, was one of many officials who feared that Chinese communities stained the map of the far-east zone an indelible yellow. The idea that East Asians were yellow, dangerous, and discernibly inferior took hold in the western imagination toward the end of nineteenth century. All around the globe, fears of the yellow race were usually attributed to a spike in the unchecked immigration of East Asians, the specter of military aggression, and economic exploitation.[40] Ever since Russian travelers and military and government officials began to take an interest in the Far East, they had no qualms in expressing their innate racial superiority vis-à-vis the yellows. Nikolai Przhevalskii, for instance, considered the Europeans a morally superior race in comparison with the "degraded inhabitants of Asia." Travels along the borderland left a particularly disagreeable impression on the influential geographer. Comparing the Chinese to the Jews, Przhevalskii observed that the

"Chinaman here is a Jew plus a Muscovite pickpocket both squared," and lamented the occasions he witnessed "Europeans being polite to this rabble."[41]

The threat of Asia's enormous population—and its deleterious influences—preoccupied many other high-ranking officials as well. The finance minister Sergei Witte conceived of the Chinese Eastern Railroad as a tool to bring together "the yellow and white races" and "open a gate for Europe into a hitherto closed off world." Much like Leland Stanford, California's first Republican governor and president of the Central Pacific Railroad, Witte deemed Chinese workers as essential for achieving national greatness. But Witte also shared Stanford's racialist sentiments. Rather than promoting integration, Witte cautioned that Russia should direct a form of segregated cohabitation between the yellow and white races.[42] The prime minister, Petr Stolypin, worried that a state without firm borders would cease to be a foreign power. "If we sleep our lethargic dreams," he warned in remarks to the Duma, the far-eastern "territories will become saturated with foreign juices, and when we awake, perhaps they will be Russian only in name."[43]

The Japanese victory over Russia in 1905 and the prospect of losing control of the Far East intensified anxieties with regard to the yellow race. Yielding an outburst of forceful reactions in the popular press, the war destabilized preconceived hierarchies. In the international arena, news agencies described the event as the first victory of the yellow race over a white people and a Christian Western empire. W. E. B. Du Bois, the influential writer and American civil rights activist, framed the war as a transformative moment in the upending of the global color line. Writing in the *Collier's Weekly*, Du Bois observed that, "for the first time in a thousand years a great white nation has measured arms with a colored nation and has been found wanting." Russia's disastrous defeat marked a sudden shift in the "hegemony of civilization" and the "awakening of the yellow races." The "magic of the word 'white' is already broken," Du Bois boldly asserted, and "the Color Line in civilization has been crossed."[44]

Russian newspapers on all sides of the political spectrum, from highbrow literary journals to the penny press intended for lower-class readers, devoted much space to covering the events, as well. But they depicted Russia's crushing defeat in the Far East largely in unflattering terms.[45] Both Tsar Nicholas II (1894–1917) and Aleksei Kuropatkin, commander-in-chief of the Russian forces, called the Japanese "short-tailed monkeys." Images of the inferior, dehumanized East Asian foe, with semi-civilized blood, threatening national security, appeared in cartoons, posters, and popular wartime prints (*lubki*). It was not uncommon for the Japanese to be associated with animals such as monkeys, rodents, or dogs. The weak, slant-eyed, yellow-skinned Japanese, standing in stark opposition to the culturally superior white-skinned Russian, acquired enormous cultural capital.[46]

In the aftermath of the Russo-Japanese War, fears of the yellow race took on heightened proportions. To allay national security concerns, mine owners experimented with race-based quotas on yellow labor, capping the number of Chinese and Korean workers at

Image 2.3 Cossacks searching for Japanese spies in a Manchurian village. The Russo–Japanese War, 1904–5, began on January 26, when Japan launched a surprise attack on Port Arthur. Approximately 31,600 Russians and 49,400 Japanese died during the war, which marked the first defeat of a major European imperialist power by an Asian nation. © Courtesy of Photo12/ Universal Images Group via Getty Images.

no more than 50 percent. It turned out, they soon learned, that the supply of Russian labor was not sufficient to keep up with the rapid economic expansion of the region. So Russian administrators invited thousands of coolies (who were paid a fraction of what Russian laborers earned) to work in the gold mines and on the railway. Desperate for cheap labor, Russian landlords and factory owners did not bother with proper paperwork. The number of Chinese workers in the gold mines increased from nearly 6,000 in 1905 to 30,400 in 1909. The Chinese played an outsized role in the expansion of the gold industry. They were also blamed for "crowding out" Russian labor and faced constant threats of expulsion. Local race prejudices widely acknowledged that cheap Chinese labor diminished product quality and posed a competitive threat to Russian workers. The Chinese, one official explained, "prey on [Russian labor]. The only thing they are concerned with is seizing as much gold as they can, as quickly as possible." The fact that the Chinese allegedly violated rules, disregarded safety procedures, and smuggled gold extracts across the border posed special problems for mine owners. "If there weren't any Chinese laborers in the gold mines," the same official concluded, "the work on the mines would proceed differently," according to a unique set of rules, as more civilized ethnic Russians gradually settled the land.[47]

In the Russian Far East, as in the United States' Far West, tens of thousands of male workers crossed the border to work in the gold mines, on farms, and on large-scale railroad projects. Little information exists about their day-to-day experiences and identities. In mines and railroads, the Chinese performed unusually strenuous work: shoveling, wheeling, and blasting rocks around the clock under challenging conditions. They endured onerous legal restrictions, racial taunts and abuse, and occasional violence—all for a fraction of the price that Russian workers commanded.[48] In the first decade of the twentieth century, and especially after the start of the Great War, the demand for Chinese and Korean labor surged in the Far East. And so did ugly racial prejudices. Pavel Unterberger, the governor-general of the Amur, blamed Russia's dependence on yellow labor for developing "idleness and drunkenness" and other bad habits. Newspapers featured sensational, often frightening, accounts of alarming descriptions of yellow labor migrants crossing the eastern border in "waves."[49]

Raw statistics did little to allay popular racial fears. In the Amur, the total number of Chinese gold miners in the workforce increased from 43 percent in 1905 to 81 percent in 1909. Administrators—without worrying about the impact on Russian economic interests—called for the expulsion of all East Asian workers without proper travel documents or residence permits. Legislation limited or attempted to prohibit the employment of yellow labor in industries and businesses. On June 21, 1910, the Duma—without specifying Chinese and Koreans directly—restricted state enterprises from hiring foreign workers. After the plague broke out in Manchuria in 1910, and subsequently spread along the railroad network, some officials lobbied to seal the Amur region entirely, on the basis that Chinese seasonal workers bore direct responsibility for bringing the deadly disease across the border. If a hard-line approach to immigration proved unrealistic to implement, the same officials requested to set up quarantine stations: to detain the Chinese for a minimum of ten days to inspect clothing, luggage, and other belongings for infectious disease. The quarantine stations segregated populations along ethnic or racial lines, with the Chinese sealed off from white Europeans or ethnic Russians in ghetto-like quarters.[50]

Despite the prohibition on yellow labor, trainloads of Chinese workers continued to cross the eastern border each month to perform essential services on farms, docks, factories, construction sites, railways, and gold mines. Patrol agents estimated that 2,236 Chinese labor migrants crossed the border in February 1914 and an additional 1,702 the following month. Nikolai L'iudvigovich Gondatti, the new governor-general of Amur, was obsessed with the idea of expelling alien labor. Sharing the view with other officials that the "Far East zone must be Russian and only for the Russians," he came to the conclusion that Chinese workers "brought nothing but harm." Due to their racial peculiarities, the Chinese saw the world differently than Russian workers and Europeans generally, with little understanding of society's legal norms and elementary sanitary standards. Undoubtedly, Gondatti observed, Chinese workers posed a public health risk by infecting Russians with infectious disease.[51] But with a labor shortage of at least four million men, the Council of Ministers on July 30, 1915, saw no choice but to ease work restrictions for Chinese and Koreans, at least on a temporary basis, irrespective of the widespread belief circulating in high-ranking circles that the yellow race was dangerous, dirty, and inassimilable.[52]

The Mass Influence of Race

Racial violence, on both the western and eastern borders of the empire, took place in the context of profound social dislocations, the appearance of exclusionary nationalist sentiment, and the rise of respectable race science. In late imperial Russia, a wide range of historical actors—from respected journalists and writers such as Fyodor Dostoevsky, Vasilii Rozanov, and Vladimir Jabotinsky to imperial administrators, journalists, and the most zealous anti-Semitic hacks—used words and images infused with racial idioms.[53] The anxieties—to say nothing of the attempts to draw hierarchies between populations—operated in a global framework, but they were always shaped by local preoccupations and power dynamics.

At the turn of the twentieth century, government officials and professional elites working in the fields of statistics, public health, crime, and disease control were not immune to the tremendous influence of racialized medical science. Some of Russia's leading scientists engaged in ideas associated with population genetics and the eugenics movement that became fashionable in liberal European settings (progressive eugenics) as well as in reactionary environments (negative eugenics). Professor Iurii Aleksandrovich Filipchenko, for instance, lectured at St. Petersburg University on Mendelian genetics, biometrics, and mutation theory, and published several well-received articles and textbooks.[54] The Ministry of the Interior was not impervious to the latest breakthroughs in criminal science infused with the language of race. In an attempt to confront recidivism and political terrorism, it relied on the techniques established by Alphonse Bertillon to detect criminals based on anthropometric measurements of the body and forensic photography. The Bertillon system was premised on the principle that all human measurements were racially fixed and obeyed statistical norms. In their descriptions of the criminal body, police officials were instructed to pay particular attention to physiognomic indicators that served as important clues to criminal identity: nose, mouth, and race or skin color.[55]

No event better illustrates the wider resonance of ideas—rooted in racial or quasi-racial language—than the sensational Beilis case. The issue of Jewish criminality, including the blood libel, had been adjudicated by Russia's courts before, but no previous case had a clear racial element. The trial of Mendel Beilis in September 1913 for the murder of Andrei Iushchinskii, a thirteen-year-old Christian boy, gave a public platform to voices operating at the margins of society. In March 1911, Iushchinskii's body was discovered in a cave in Kiev's Lukianovka district, punctured with numerous stab wounds in the head and upper torso. The corpse was drained of vast quantities of blood. It did not take long for rumors to circulate that the Jews had committed the crime as a blood ritual to bake matzo. Organizations with deep loyalty to the monarchy and an intense interest in promulgating conspiracy theories and zealous anti-Semitism picked up on the case. *Dvuglavyi orel* (The Double-Headed Eagle), a newspaper operated by a radical right student youth league, proclaimed that "there is no doubt whatsoever that we have here a case of ritual murder carried out by the kikes," and that the murder was part of a racial conspiracy to destroy the "weak, helpless, and oppressed" Russian Orthodox masses.[56]

What was once regarded as an irrational obsession associated with medieval times, the Jewish ritual murder accusation found new life in nineteenth-century Europe, including Russia. As other high-profile ritual murder trials in Central Europe, the drama of the Beilis case played out in the open courtroom, informed by modern legal and criminal norms and the language of science.[57] The outspoken psychiatrist Sikorskii served as one of the star witnesses for the prosecution. Over the years, Sikorskii had acquired a reputation as a prominent public intellectual and an expert in the field of race science. His writings were often marked by excessive, unusually tasteless rhetoric. In his numerous publications—from his analysis of the poet Aleksandr Pushkin's blackness to his work on the Russian race-nation—Sikorskii placed Jews at the very bottom of a racial hierarchy, equating them with American "Negro elements," whose racial peculiarity was characterized by a wild instinct and crude sensuality.[58]

After examining Iushchinskii's body, Sikorskii determined that the murder was an act of Jewish "racial vengeance." At the trial, Sikorskii went further by proclaiming that the ritual murder of Christian children would continue while "there is agitation by races that nourish savagery among their members and while we [Christians] are unable to take measures to liberate ourselves from them."[59] It did not take long for the trial to erupt in an international cause célèbre, where Sikorskii's expert scientific analysis of the boy's body, as well as other aspects of the case, were made public. Although the jury eventually absolved Beilis of the crime, it nevertheless determined that the murder was committed with ritual intent. Special correspondents writing for newspapers around the world—from the esteemed *New York Times* and *Times of London* to the widely disseminated *Novoe vremia* and the extreme-right press—reported on every detail of the case, including the jury's ambiguous verdict. While the *Times of London* and many other papers in Russia and the United States denounced the split decision, the *Dvuglavyi orel* rejoiced: "The torturers of Christian children exult, but [the Jews'] criminality has been proven with exhaustive clarity in court."[60]

Several months after the jury handed down its verdict in the Beilis case, Russia entered World War I. The mass violence had far-reaching repercussions in daily life. In Russia, as in Britain and Germany, the war intensified racial prejudices already evident in the prewar years. With more than ten million men conscripted in 1914 and 1915, the Great War had disastrous consequences for Russia's farms, factories, and industries, including on the Sino-Russian frontier. At a time of radical emergency, Poles, Germans, Chinese, and Jews all suffered denunciations for their alleged disloyalty to the imperial Russian state. More than 400,000 Jews served in the armed forces, but top military officials and the radical right agitated to banish Jews from the military ranks for their "unusually harmful" ways. It was not uncommon for military officials to describe Jews as "weak," "prone to bribery," and "disloyal."[61] The army used its vast powers to launch campaigns against suspected enemy aliens and spies. Jews, Germans, and Chinese were subject to unusually cruel attacks, including mass deportations and arrests, accompanied by widespread rumors of disloyalty.[62] Under direct orders from the General Staff, the Russian army deported as many as half a million Jews from the eastern front, including large regions of the northwestern parts of the Pale of Settlement. The mass ethnic deportations were often accompanied by looting, rioting, rape, and murder.

As a deep conservatism gripped Russian culture and politics, Jews emerged as the most visible threat to the health and prosperity of the imperial Russian nation. Yet, to argue that Jews proved to be *the* exception in an otherwise tolerant imperial order is to overlook the very problematic meanings of Russianness and the ways in which differences were constructed, defined, and maintained. Various other populations, including Poles, Chinese, Koreans, and Japanese, experienced similar frustrations, burdens, and attacks due to their perceived differences. Race science offered what appeared to be an objective rationale to keep dangerous and inferior groups in their place. This does not mean that the concept of race—a notoriously slippery, malleable construct—always carried the day, inspired collective action, or superseded religious or economic formulations (it did not). But considerable evidence exists that, as the empire crumbled under its own weight, racial thinking began to filter down to the public by way of a complex system of signs, symbols, and ideas.

CHAPTER 3
"THE MOST HOPEFUL NATION ON EARTH"

In November 1922, Claude McKay, the Jamaican-born American writer of peasant origins, participated in the Fourth Congress of the Communist International, or Comintern. Established to promote world revolution by advancing an anti-colonial and anti-racist agenda, the Comintern strove to become the global party of the proletariat. A total of 343 voting delegates, representing fifty-eight countries, gathered for four weeks in Moscow and Petrograd (renamed Leningrad in 1924). The Fourth Congress was tasked to lay the groundwork for massive resistance to fascism, to work on women's liberation, and to investigate anti-colonial struggles, including the Negro problem. McKay traveled to the Soviet Union to escape what he described in his autobiography, *A Long Way from Home*, as the "suffocating ghetto of color consciousness."[1]

At the opening of the congress convened at the historic Bolshoi Theatre, McKay sat beside Grigory Zinoviev, the official chair of the Communist International, and delivered a spirited speech on the plight of American racism. McKay's dark skin color—his unmistakable African features, including unusually high, arching eyebrows, and bright smile—fit the Comintern's crude conception of model blackness. According to McKay's recollections of the events, "Russians wanted a typical Negro at the Congress." It turned out that Otto Huiswood, the official delegate of the American Workers Party of America, did not meet Soviet racial ideals. Huiswood, unlike McKay, was too "yellow" in complexion to serve as the face of Soviet propaganda.[2]

Image 3.1 Grigory Zinoviev, Claude McKay, and Nikolai Bukharin in Moscow, circa 1923. © Courtesy of Claude McKay Collection. Yale Collection of American Literature, Beinecke Rare Book and Manuscript Library.

By all accounts, McKay enjoyed exceptional status in the Soviet Union. He remembered the visit fondly. "Photographs of his black face," McKay recounted, were soon "everywhere among the highest Soviet rulers, in the principal streets, adorning the walls of the city." "Never in my life did I feel prouder of being an African, a black, and no mistake about it."[3] McKay spent six months in the Soviet Union, primarily in Petrograd and Moscow, touring military bases and publishing articles, poems, and stories in the Soviet press on the historical complexity of American race relations. When he returned home, W. E. B. Du Bois invited McKay to publish his impressions in *The Crisis*, the official magazine of the National Association of the Advancement of Colored People (NAACP). To Russians, McKay observed, he appeared "merely another type," an exotic curiosity. "I could not detect a trace of ignorant snobbishness among the educated classes, and the attitude of the common workers, the soldiers and sailors, was still more remarkable. It was so beautifully naïve; for them I was only a black member of the world of humanity."[4]

McKay was one of hundreds of African Americans who traveled to the Soviet Union to witness the transformation of a new age. After seizing power in October 1917, the Bolshevik party spent considerable resources promoting its commitment to fighting racial oppression in global affairs. The revolution emancipated peasants from the power of landowners, soldiers and generals from the authority of autocratic generals, and workers from the arbitrary will of the capitalists. The Declaration of the Rights of the Peoples of Russia, issued on November 2, 1917, promised the "abolition of any and all national and national-religious privileges and disabilities," the "free development of national minorities," and the right to self-determination.[5] As the doctrines of white solidarity swept the globe—from South Africa to North America and Australasia—Communist Russia emerged as the most hopeful nation on earth for its commitment to racial equality and human rights.[6]

The Pitfalls of Revolution

The revolution promised a new political order rooted in social progress, the advancement of history, and the assurances of a just life, but the utopian visions were quickly submerged in flames. Approximately 15.5 million people, or 9 percent of the population, perished in the civil war, resulting in one of the greatest demographic catastrophes in Russian history. Some died as a result of mass violence, many others from disease, hunger, and the hardships of everyday life. Between 1918 and 1922, as many as five million people succumbed to starvation. With the economy in a free fall, food production ceased to function. Prices on basic staples rose precipitously, including on bread, meats, eggs, sugar, fuel, and raw materials. The women, men, and children caught up in the enormous social dislocations caused by war, revolution, and civil war experienced unparalleled trauma and brutality.[7]

Ukraine—a politically and territorially volatile region, covering roughly the southwestern provinces of the Russian Empire and the eastern section of Austria-Hungary—was particularly hard hit. The civil war in Ukraine witnessed the total breakdown of authority. The military conflict precipitated the inversion of hierarchies and the collapse of civilizational norms and social inhibitions. When the Germans withdrew from Kiev on December 14, 1918, Symon Petliura, Ataman in Chief of the warlords comprising the Ukrainian armies, vied with several other military groups to establish control over the Ukrainian lands. Political actors on all sides of the military conflict—from the Directorate of Ukraine and its allies to the Reds, Whites, Polish legionnaires, and peasant bandits—practiced extreme violence. Violence, in 1919 and 1920, was not only the work of soldiers or paramilitary units; civilian populations with intimate knowledge of one another joined in the bloodshed, as well.[8]

The military operations—the ruthless attacks and counterattacks by all protagonists involved in the conflict, coupled with the rise of militant nationalism—caused unprecedented mass casualties. The Jewish community suffered unparalleled bloodshed. According to the most conservative estimates, no fewer than 50,000 Jews died as a result of 1,500 pogroms in some 1,300 localities. In all likelihood, the mortality rate was much higher, destabilizing virtually all aspects of Jewish communal existence in Ukraine and, in some cases, systematically eliminating entire communities. Some scholars have estimated that the violence accounted for as many as 150,000 deaths, with an additional 200,000 individuals wounded or crippled, 300,000 children orphaned, and 100,000 spouses widowed. Wartime conditions uprooted tens of thousands of Jews from their homes. Many of the refugees suffered attacks as they roamed the countryside in search of shelter or new homes. The dramatic social crises accompanying the fighting—the rise in typhus and other epidemic disease, chronic shortages, and ravaging hunger – caused numerous additional deaths. In all, according to the Russian Red Cross Committee to Aid Victims of Pogroms, one million Jews may have suffered as a consequence of the events of the 1918–1921 period.[9]

Politically and operationally, the mass carnage was the product of a new paramilitary violence that broke out in much of Central and Eastern Europe. The wartime pogroms were typically carried out by trained soldiers or paramilitary units, intent on identifying and exterminating Jewish or Jewish-looking subjects. The violence toward Jews was not isolated or accidental. The goal, in other words, was not only to terrorize, humiliate, and plunder, but also to ethnically cleanse, or physically remove, all remnants of Jewish life.[10] In Proskurov, Cossacks—forming the core of the White Army detachments— divided themselves in small groups in search of Jews. The pogrom lasted approximately four hours, resulting in at least 1,500 casualties (some sources identified as many as 4,000 deaths). Relying mostly on knives and bayonets, the Cossacks slaughtered men, women, children, and the elderly in the most barbaric fashion. In Bobruisk, Polish soldiers murdered Jews for counterrevolutionary activities, burying the bodies in mass graves. Similar military-style operations occurred in town after town across the southwestern borderlands.[11]

Amid the coordinated attacks against Jews, military units pillaged Jewish belongings, humiliated and terrorized unarmed civilians, and carried out sexual violence against Jewish women and girls. A great deal of the violence against Jewish civilians was sanctioned from above, as part of a free-for-all struggle to control the Ukrainian lands. But with the collapse of state authority, it was often challenging to distinguish perpetrators from trusted allies. Long-lasting communal relationships self-destructed at a moment's notice. Civilian populations committed mass violence against their neighbors, usually for purely mercenary reasons. Peasants torched Jewish homes, including houses of worship, plundered Jewish belongings, and organized mass violence – in some cases, helping military units to eradicate all signs of Jewish communal life.[12]

In July 1918, the Bolshevik leadership articulated its position on pogroms and anti-Semitism more generally. The Council of People's Commissars (Sovnarkom), or the executive authority of the new revolutionary regime, instructed "all Soviet institutions to take uncompromising measures to tear the antisemitic movement out by the roots."[13] Vladimir Lenin (1917–24) and the Bolsheviks saw anti-Jewish persecution in essentially counterrevolutionary terms—as an attempt to destroy the political legitimacy of the party in an effort to restore Tsarist rule. To eradicate anti-Semitism, organizations disseminated leaflets, published newspaper articles, and coordinated educational work. Lenin's March 1919 speech on pogroms, recorded on a gramophone, played widely in workplaces, agitational-political trains, and political demonstrations. "Only the most ignorant and downtrodden people," Lenin proclaimed, "can believe the lies and slander that are spread about the Jews."[14]

The Soviet state condemned anti-Jewish behavior—including pogroms and ritual murder allegations—not as crimes against the Jewish people per se (the Soviet Criminal Code did not include anti-Semitism as an official category), but as crimes against the legitimacy of the Soviet state. Bolsheviks promoted enlightened propaganda to debunk the evils of religious fanaticism and superstitious behavior, including the ritual murder tale. They set up revolutionary tribunals to punish anti-Semitic or counterrevolutionary behavior. A handful of individuals received sentences ranging from solitary confinement up to six months to execution by firing squad for the worst offenses. Jews, in hopes of resolving social conflicts, turned to Soviet institutions for justice: to revenge the murder of family members or to reclaim belongings taken over by their neighbors. Occasionally, Soviet officials administered elaborate trials to discipline anti-Jewish activities, as they did in Moscow in 1922, when an elderly Jewish man was accused of ritual murder. The police wound up arresting the old man (a member of the Jewish burial society) for carrying the corpse of a recently deceased boy from the morgue to the local cemetery. The court ruled that the Jewish man was the victim of "prejudice," for which the three accusers were severely reprimanded.[15]

Black Visitors

Contemporary observers had long compared the experiences of the Jews of Tsarist Russia with those of Black Americans. In an article entitled "Lessons from Russia," published in *The Crisis* before the outbreak of the Great War, the celebrated economist Isaac Max Rubinow noted that the Jew in Russia, much like the Negro in Jim Crow America, was considered an "outlaw under the law," with Jews laughed and sneered at by the members of the Slavic race. "A specific

Jewish crime has been invented in Russia—now that sounds quite familiar, does it not?—though the Jewish crime—ritual murder—is altogether the product of a wild imagination. And pogroms happen in Russia and are as brutal or worse even than lynching is in the South."[16]

The Black American community, with support from Rubinow and other like-minded Jews from the Pale of Settlement, did not hide its disdain for Tsarist reactionary policies. Black journalists referred to the predominantly Black neighborhood as a "ghetto," a term usually associated with Jewish poverty and segregation in Tsarist Russia.[17] Black Americans organized fundraising efforts and demonstrations to protest Russia's treatment of Jews. They published articles and opinion pieces to voice their concerns, usually in newspapers with modest print runs. The *Cleveland Gazette* was one of a handful of Black newspapers that felt Russia "treated [Jews] worse than our [Black] people in the South have ever been," while a Black Chicago magazine scornfully observed that Russia was "the most barbaric and corrupt government on the face of the globe."[18]

The October Revolution changed Russia's image on the world stage. The scientists, engineers, farmers, artists, thinkers, and writers who visited the Soviet state were inspired by a vision of world revolution that liberated humanity. Black Americans, in particular, looked to Soviet Russia as a place where they would not be judged by the color of their skin. Du Bois read stories in newspapers about the harrowing aspects of the Soviet experiment: from the collapse of industry and famine to homelessness and emotional despair. In late summer of 1926, at the age of fifty-eight, he traveled across the Atlantic, on what would be the first of four trips, to investigate. With stops in Moscow, Leningrad, Nizhni Novgorod (Gorky), Kiev, and Odessa, Du Bois had the occasion to visit schools, universities, factories, and stores, as well as palaces, museums, and libraries. In an unpublished work based on his travels to the Soviet Union, entitled *Russia and America: An Interpretation*, Du Bois asserted that he had witnessed poverty and misery—the "hordes of incredibly dirty, ragged and wild children of war and famine" and the "long lines of ragged people, waiting to buy a loaf of bread"—but that he was also struck by the sheer enthusiasm for revolution. Du Bois felt that his own travails trained him to know what racial discrimination looked like:

> I have seen Irishmen crawling out of the filth of their bogs to step in my face and crow; hillbillies and crackers from Alabama and Arkansas could spit on me to the applause of thousands; German peasants newly free could insult me; and Italians and Slovaks and a thousand others could not only deprive me of a living but depend on white American mobs and police to jail or even lynch me for protesting.[19]

The Soviet Union, by contrast, did not restrict its citizens in terms of where they could sleep, eat, study, or use a public bathroom because of skin color or nationality.

The visit made an enormous impression upon the civil rights activist. Upon his return to America, Du Bois characterized the new Soviet state in *The Crisis* as "astonishing and new and of fateful importance to the future of civilization."[20] In *Russia and America*, Du Bois expanded his views. Intimately linking racial politics with autobiographical experience, he declared that Soviet Russia was "the only modern country where people are not more or less taught and encouraged to despise and look down on some group or race. I know countries where race and color prejudice show only slight manifestations, but no countries where race and color prejudice [seem] so absolutely absent." Du Bois approached the Soviet experiment through the historical experiences of "ten million American Negroes." In America, he was met with "everything from curiosity to insult," but in the Soviet Union, Du Bois recalled with fondness, "women sit beside me quite [confidently] and unconsciously."[21]

William L. Patterson, a civil rights activist and the son of a former slave, had a similar experience. Patterson traveled to the Soviet Union under the auspices of the Communist Party Workers' School to study in The Communist University of Toilers of the East (KUTV). Founded in 1921, the Moscow-based university prepared students from the East for revolutionary work. For more than fifteen years, the university served as a pipeline for launching the careers of influential scholars, artists, and political figures in Africa, Asia, and Latin America. In his autobiography, Patterson remembered the tremendous exhilaration he felt in moving past the biases of race and class that were ominously present in the United States. In Moscow, Patterson concluded, an American Negro "looks at, talks to, works with white men and women and youth as an equal. It is as if one had suffered with a painful affliction for many years and had suddenly awakened to discover that the pain had gone. The Russians seemed to give a man's skin coloration only a descriptive value."[22]

Patterson's future wife, Louise Thompson, a social activist and a leading organizer of the highly publicized Soviet propaganda film, *Black and White*, about race relations in the American South, reflected in an interview with a journalist that "Russia was the only place where I was able to forget that I was a Negro."[23] On another occasion, Thompson commented that "we come from a country where everything is denied us—work, protection of life and property, freedom to go where we will and to live where we will—where we are despised and humiliated at every turn. And here [in the USSR] we are accorded every courtesy—free to go where we will and eagerly welcomed—given every opportunity to enjoy ourselves and to travel—free to pursue any work that we choose."[24]

Soviet racial enlightenment inspired dozens of Black Americans to make the transatlantic pilgrimage to the Soviet Union. Their numbers, along with the parade of highly skilled workers and sympathizers, steadily increased in the late 1920s. They came not as unwitting dupes of Communist propaganda, but as active participants in the shaping of the new Soviet regime.[25] Some were drawn to the Soviet Union by the prospects of earning a decent wage, others hoped to study in institutions of higher learning and to help build the world's first socialist society. Most went for short visits, a handful married white Russian women and decided to stay for longer stretches of time.[26]

One such figure was Harry Haywood, who, after witnessing the bloody race riot in Chicago in July 1919, committed himself to struggling "against whatever it was that made racism possible." Haywood rejected Black nationalism, as well as the politics of the NAACP for its "blind acceptance of white middle-class values and culture," and, instead, joined the American Communist Party. Along with several other Black Americans, he enrolled in KUTV and continued his studies of political economy, historical materialism, and the history of the Communist Party at the International Lenin School. Haywood stayed long enough in the Soviet Union to marry Ekaterina (Ina), a white ballerina student with a nice command of English, although it does not appear that the couple lived together long, if at all, save for occasional weekend trysts at Ina's mother apartment. Over the years, Haywood tried, unsuccessfully, to bring Ina back to the United States, but eventually lost contact with her after several attempts. Among other things, it turned out that Haywood's divorce papers from his first marriage in America were not finalized.[27]

At a time of severe economic shortages, to say nothing of long bread lines, most Black visitors lived comfortably in the Soviet Union. They received perks such as free housing, food, clothing, weekly allowances, and all-expense paid vacations to the Black Sea. High-profile visitors received a warm reception, with unparalleled access to important political and cultural figures. The poet Langston Hughes and the actor Wayland Rudd were "lionized no end" and "introduced [at cultural gatherings] as representatives of the great Negro people," according to Hughes's highly stylized memoir, *I Wonder as I Wander*. Along with Rudd, Louise Thompson, and nineteen other Black Americans, Hughes traveled to the Soviet Union in 1932 to make the film, *Black and White*. The group, treated as honored guests, resided in a luxurious hotel one block from the Kremlin. Hughes gloated that his salary, "in terms of Russian buying power," was "about a hundred times a week as much as [he] had ever made anywhere else."[28]

Anti-racism was at the very core of official Soviet state policy. And it is not all that surprising that the small colony of Black American visitors generated a great deal of media attention. By the time the New Economy Policy collapsed in 1928, a vast propaganda campaign elevated the status of Black Communists in the global project of building socialism. Educational and artistic resources—including photographs and drawings in the mass press—were deployed to promote Soviet racial enlightenment and to abolish racist stereotypes. The Sixth Congress of the Comintern adopted a resolution in 1928 that placed African Americans at the center of a "fight against all forms of white chauvinism." Consequently, Soviet visual culture depicted Black Americans not in exotic sensual stereotypes, but as oppressed victims of capitalism or as conscious political subjects.[29] The well-publicized project, lasting approximately until the 1960s, condemned US racism, while glorifying the Soviet Union's commitment to racial justice and human rights. Newspaper articles, photographs, children's stories, pamphlets, literature (in translation), and graphic art reinforced the message of Soviet exceptionalism and moral superiority in the struggle against global racial oppression.[30]

The Scottsboro case—when nine African American teenagers, ranging in age from thirteen to nineteen, were falsely accused of group raping two white prostitutes on a freight train in May 1931—became an international symbol of white racial oppression. More than two hundred demonstrations against the injustices of the rape trial were organized throughout Europe, Latin America, and South Africa. By the time Langston Hughes and his group traveled to the Soviet Union, the case had become an international cause célèbre. The American Communist Party capitalized on the hysteria of the Scottsboro case to recruit Black Americans, while Soviet journalists, writers, and graphic artists exposed the hypocrisy of American racist violence and segregation. Dmitri Moor's cartoon—first published on the front page of *Komsomol'skaia pravda* [Komsomol Truth], the official organ of the Communist Youth Organization, and subsequently reprinted widely—depicted a white American capitalist, painted in gold, green, and black, masquerading as the Statue of Liberty, in the service of white supremacy. The greedy male capitalist holds an electric chair in his right hand, with the Scottsboro boys, shown in austere black and white, shackled by their wrists awaiting execution.[31]

In a society committed to the ideals of internationalism, race was never absent. Black students in Comintern schools complained that they were called "monkeys" or were laughed at or spit on because of their skin color. One student from a French African colony complained that he had experienced more racism in Moscow than in other capitalist countries: "No one spat at me there [Italy or India] the way they do here in Moscow."[32] Despite these and other similar

Image 3.2 "Freedom to the prisoners of Scottsboro!" Soviet propaganda poster, drawing by Dmitri Moor, 1932. © Courtesy of Ne Boltai!

anecdotal incidents, Black visitors to the Soviet Union were typically perceived as objects of curiosity. In his autobiography, Haywood, echoing several Black American visitors, noted that his skin color was seen as something strange and different. "Children followed us in the streets," Haywood recalled. "If we paused to greet a friend, we found ourselves instantly surrounded by curious crowds—unabashedly staring at us."[33] Other Black Americans noted that they were mistaken for Uzbeks or other Central Asian peoples, although "a little bigger and a little darker than most."[34] Ultimately, the promises of constructing a post-racial order proved challenging to carry out. Soviet racial scorn, it turned out, was directed not at Black visitors—the face of global racial injustice—but at fellow citizens in its own backyard.

Labeling People

A new approach to nationality policy accompanied the Soviet narrative on racism and anti-racism. The Bolsheviks took over an expansive land and a multiethnic and a multilingual population. The goal of early Soviet state policy was to develop class loyalties, while doing away with separatist nationalism and oppression. Promising national self-determination or what Joseph Stalin called "real rights in the localities [the populations] inhabit," the new government in power worked to restructure the former empire as a federation of republics established along ethnic political units, committed to the ideals of internationalism and the universal desire for equal rights. By 1922, the Bolshevik party succeeded in consolidating much of the former empire into the Union of Soviet Socialist Republics. Portions of the northwestern borderlands (Latvia, Lithuania, and Estonia), the principality of Finland, the Congress of Poland, and sections of the southwestern borderlands remained outside of the official Soviet borders as constituted at the time. In due time, these territories would bear the brunt of state-sponsored paranoia, targeting presumed foreign collaborators and alleged threats to state security.[35]

In the years following the revolution, the Bolsheviks, grounded in Marxist ideology, remained highly suspicious of national self-expression. This did not stop them from supporting policies that strengthened the national consciousness of ethnic minorities—many of whom were deemed backward—while helping overcome long-standing group prejudices. The Bolshevik party viewed national self-expression in paradoxical terms, as an unavoidable transitional period to a new international socialist order. To transform the old empire into a multinational socialist state, it ratified, in 1923, a series of resolutions promoting the development of distinct national cultures, languages, and territories. The idea was that national identities would eventually coexist peacefully with Soviet socialist culture and that all ethnic groups would have equal legal rights, with the expression of ethnic violence punishable by law.

The Soviet Union took the lead in sponsoring highly contradictory affirmative action policies and programs explicitly benefiting certain ethnic groups or nationalities that had suffered discrimination under the Tsarist regime.[36] To implement the experiment, the state relied on the category of nationality. The results were remarkable on many levels. At breakneck speed, literacy, schools, and cultural expression in native languages were promoted, including literature, movies, newspapers, journals, and theater; new alphabets were established; and members of local nationalities were promoted to key leadership positions, in many cases replacing ethnic Russians.

What constituted nationality? At the outset, the question was fraught with disagreements. In contrast to the prerevolutionary era, Soviet censuses moved away from native language and religion as the essential components of nationality. Census takers relied on the direct testimony of respondents to determine the nationality to which they belonged. The First All-Union Census, conducted in 1926, counted some 172 official nationalities.[37] The Soviet state used the category of nationality—along with markers such as class, sex, and age—to delineate rights, resources, and obligations. Citizens were constantly required to record their nationality. Job applications, school and university registration forms, medical papers, and various other documentary records all had a line marked for nationality.[38]

The internal passport, introduced officially in December 1932, became the single most powerful tool for ascribing nationality.

Originally, the law on passports and the registration of urban residents (what came to be known as the *propiska*) was intended to improve population counts by controlling the flow of peasants from villages to cities. In the period 1928–32, as many as twelve million peasants left the countryside. Some cities in the industrial heartland of the Dnepr-Donbas region of Ukraine and the Urals trebled in population, while established cities witnessed the influx of a steady stream of labor migrants, attracted by the prospects of working in heavy industry.[39] Passports helped stem the flow of illegal internal migration. As time went on, the documents proved particularly useful for carrying out police sweeps—removing populations from urban areas not engaged in industrial or socially useful work; identifying and purging socially harmful or alien elements; searching apartment buildings; sentencing people for criminal violations; and gathering compromising information.[40]

All citizens of the Soviet Union over the age of sixteen and permanent residents in cities and workers' settlements, in state farms,

Image 3.3 The internal passport of Leonid Brezhnev, the General Secretary of the Communist Party, issued on June 11, 1947, with the nationality recorded as Ukrainian. © Courtesy of Laski Diffusion/Getty Images.

and at new construction sites were issued internal passports. By the late 1930s, the passport system (which remained in effect until the collapse of the Soviet Union) was employed in all major Soviet cities, industrial centers, and border zones, with some 50 million people out of approximately 162 million acquiring the document. Soviet passports listed the individual's name, age, sex, social position, permanent residence, place of employment, and nationality (on the fifth line). This information contributed significantly to an individual's right of movement and residence, the ability to find gainful employment, and access to goods.

Nationality served as an important factor in how the Soviet state assigned, but also limited, populations' rights and resources. Beginning in 1938, the People's Commissariat for Internal Affairs (NKVD) stipulated that nationality was no longer the free choice of the individual but was determined by the nationality of the parents. One of the unintended consequences of the state-driven policies— and the emergence of an exceedingly complicated registration system in the 1930s and beyond—was the indoctrination of the belief that each individual's nationality was preserved and inherited for posterity. As we will see in the pages to follow, the fixing of nationality in the internal passport played a vital role in the systematic persecution of populations by ethnic criteria.[41]

In official pronouncements, the Bolshevik party denounced the logic of racial thinking. Favoring the view that culture was a product of the environment, Soviet social scientists shared with their French colleagues an interest in neo-Lamarckian theories of inheritance. In their study of race and culture, Soviet scientific experts and government administrators, steeped in the science of Marxism-Leninism, worked to counter the Nazi propaganda machine. Racial traits, they asserted, were not fixed or eternal but were associated with distinct stages of historical development and socioeconomic processes.

Some scholars have argued that the valorization of the Marxist-sociological method in social-scientific thought and government policy—that a person was not tainted irrevocably by his or her biological origins—helps to explain an important difference between the two totalitarian regimes: why Soviet mass terror took on different forms than that of Nazi Germany. According to this line of argument, Soviet violence of the 1930s and beyond did not set as its goal the total extermination of populations as an object in itself.[42] More recent scholarship has pointed out that the Nazi regime presents itself as a rather extreme test case in determining the presence or absence of race in the Soviet Union.[43] From a comparative perspective, it might be more useful to situate the Third Reich, along with Jim Crow America and apartheid South Africa, on one end of a continuum of racial regimes, and the Soviet Union somewhere on the other end. Soviet racial logics, in other words, were part of broader ideas, practices, and policies in circulation at the time.[44]

Despite formally rejecting biological paradigms, the Soviet Union reproduced the structures and practices of race in surprising ways. As Joseph Stalin (1927–53) consolidated political power in the late 1920s, ethnic hostility gradually replaced class-enemy antagonism. The Soviet Union's racist ideas and policies played out most forcefully in the geopolitically sensitive border zones. In 1928, officials determined to cleanse all unreliable ethnic and national groups from its borders. The measures took several years to implement, and by 1938, according to the most detailed archival study of ethnic cleansing, the operations targeted around 800,000 politically unreliable elements for forcible deportation.[45] In most cases, military-style executions accompanied the forcible relocation of enemy nations. At first, the Bolshevik operations zeroed in on its international borders. By the summer of 1937, at the height of the Great Terror, the security police expanded its work. No longer bound by geography, the systematic removal and physical annihilation of hostile ethnic groups was at the core of the Stalinist terror campaign. As Stalinism continued to imagine new conspiracies and enemy categories, the lines between social and ethnic categories, center and periphery were difficult to distinguish with certainty.

The threat of war with Nazi Germany, Poland, and other neighboring states furthered suspicions of foreign espionage by capitalist governments. Fears of internal enemies and devastating defeats in the early phases of the war resulted in the systematic repression of non-Russian nationalities. Stalin appealed to the Soviet people to protect the fatherland and to root out deserters, purveyors of false rumors, spies, and saboteurs. The war witnessed an important shift in ethnic cleansing practices: from the partial deportation of populations in sensitive border regions to the cleansing of entire groups of people regardless of location.[46]

The Red Army relied on ethnic categories as noted in passports and other documentary records to remove, deport, and imprison stigmatized nationalities. Special forces supervised high-security areas, which ran along the entirety of the international land and sea borders of the Soviet Union. Soviet authorities imposed rigid controls over its borders, with little movement in and out of the country permitted. In the western borderlands, diaspora nationalities with strong cross-border ties—Germans, Finns, Poles, Estonians, Latvians—were targeted for ethnic purification. Mass violence often accompanied the forcible relocations. Around half of the German and Polish population was removed or physically eliminated from Ukraine; thousands of Finns, Estonians, and Latvians were relocated to Siberia and Central Asia from the Leningrad border region; and in 1940, nearly 10 percent of the population in Soviet-occupied Poland—approximately 200,000 Poles and 60,000 Jews—were deported to Central Asia.[47]

Similar mass terror campaigns, defined largely in ethnic terms, played out along the eastern and southern border zones. The Japanese invasion of Manchuria, which started a fourteen-year war with China, put the Soviets on high alert. In September 1931, Moscow began to shift its security concerns to the Far East. On the Soviet side of the border, Soviets deployed vast resources, stationing more than 800,000 soldiers east of Lake Baikal and around 700,000 troops in Manchukuo. With cross-border contacts cut off, the secret police intensified its search for spies and undesirable elements.[48] The suspicions against East Asians intensified with the threat of war with Japan, resulting in the expulsion of almost all Chinese migrant workers and Korean tenant farmers. In fact, the Korean population, numbering at least 37,000 families (or some 175,000 people) may have suffered the most in the mass repressions. Between 1935 and 1938, the NKVD forcibly relocated by train all ethnic Koreans from the Far East to Kazakhstan, Turkmenistan, and Uzbekistan, accounting for around one quarter of the total population targeted for removal.[49] At the height of the war, in the summer of 1942, Soviet leadership turned its attention to the southern periphery, a region with a predominantly Muslim population that had long been perceived as a security threat. By 1944, the Soviets resettled approximately half a million Chechens and Ingush from the North Caucasus in Central Asia.[50]

The internal passport system facilitated the creation of a human Soviet archive: an exhaustive process that entailed the cataloguing of the population in toto. Registration was not always a model of efficiency. Descriptive notations could be altered or forged. Identity documents could be procured on the black market for the right price. Police officers often failed to maintain up-to-date files of passports and residence registration. In some instances, hundreds of citizens could live in a region without being officially registered. But for all its faults and loopholes, the internal passport document—with the nationality clearly marked on the fifth line—facilitated the systematic identification, removal, and, in some cases, physical execution of entire populations by ethnic criteria.[51] The decision to inscribe the ethnicity of every individual drastically redefined how populations viewed themselves and interacted with the world around them. This system also went a long way in priming people to think in racial terms.[52]

Soviet Anti-Semitism

In 1928, the Soviet regime came up with an outlandishly unique attempt to solve the Jewish problem. Birobidzhan—a sparsely populated land along the Manchurian border—was designed as an autonomous district, or a new center for Jewish life, rooted in socialist principles, rivaling Zionism's invention of a modern nation-state in Middle East Palestine. From a geopolitical perspective, the remote territory served as a buffer against Japanese imperial expansion. The idea was to create a Soviet agricultural colony where Yiddish would be the primary language and where Jews would move into agricultural labor and other so-called productive economic sectors. To attract new settlers, the government provided discounted travel, food subsidies, tax exemptions, and other perquisites. By the mid-1930s, schools, newspapers, publishing houses, and other Jewish institutions were set up. The Soviets did not forcibly relocate large numbers of Jews to Birobidzhan, as they did other unreliable national minority populations to border zones. Only a limited number of Jewish activists made the long voyage. The sparsely populated region in the Far East failed to live up to its ambitions as a secular cultural mecca for proletarian Jewish life and culture.[53]

Despite the failures of the Birobidzhan project, Jews were among the prime beneficiaries of Soviet nationality policies. Unlike in the prerevolutionary era, Jews under the Soviets were not subject to official quotas or restrictions on their mobility. The influx of Jews to Moscow, Leningrad, Kiev, Kharkov, Minsk, and other large cities in the Soviet Union coincided with an explosion of urban growth. The 1939 census counted some three million Jewish residents, one-third of whom were first-generation immigrants in places outside the former Pale of Settlement. The process of acculturating to Soviet norms was by no means straightforward or painless. While many first-generation Soviet Jews remained committed to religious traditions and ways of life, others took advantage of all that the Soviet state had to offer.[54] In less than one generation, upward mobility turned out to be a stunning success. Jews climbed atop the sprawling Soviet bureaucracy, becoming highly visible members of the Communist Party and the Red Army. Jews were drawn to institutions of secondary and higher learning, comprising more than three and a half times the Jewish share of the population. No less impressive, Jews made up a disproportionate number of Soviet doctors, dentists, journalists, scientists, university professors, and musicians. In the most prominent universities, the number of Jewish students skyrocketed as well, with the greatest disparities in four specific areas of specialization: medicine, economics, music, and the arts.[55]

The spectacular climb atop the Soviet social ladder was not without challenges. As a global economic crisis erupted, the Stalinist regime attacked Jewish institutions with renewed ferocity. Beginning in 1928, with Stalin and his close circle of political allies steeped in delusional, conspiratorial thinking about the dangers of the capitalist world, the rate of anti-Semitic incidents ticked up.[56] The Stalinist state, in contrast to Germany or Poland of the 1930s, did not allow anti-Semitism to become the guiding ideological principle of the land. Under Stalin, at least until the start of World War II, officials continued to condemn anti-Semitism: to speak publicly against the perils of anti-Jewish attitudes and behavior.

But in a period of economic and political turbulence, anti-Jewish sentiment reared its ugly head in a variety of settings. Jews were particularly vulnerable to abuse at factories, schools and universities, and on shop floors. The Soviets closed down all independent Jewish political parties and Jewish institutions; disbanded the Jewish sections of the Communist Party known as Evsektsii; and blamed Jews for basic goods shortages and the precipitous surge in consumer prices. In Belarus, drunken hooligans intimidated and occasionally beat up Jewish-looking shopkeepers, pedestrians, and train passengers. It was not uncommon for Jewish students to experience physical violence. A member of the communist youth organization known as the Komsomol reported that his peers ordered him to take off his pants to verify if he was circumcised. Similar incidents of harassment and intimidation took place all across the Soviet Union. One Jewish violinist of the Bolshoi Theater committed suicide after the artistic director, Nikolai Golovanov, repeatedly harassed him for his Jewishness. Some towns in Ukraine even witnessed murderous anti-Semitic riots.[57]

The war with Nazi Germany exacerbated interethnic conflicts. The German forces attacked the Soviet Union on June 22, 1941. Hitler saw Germany's eastern frontier largely in colonial terms: a vast space that could be controlled at will on the basis of mythic notions of race. To construct a hierarchical order, the territories were to be liquidated of Jews and other racial enemies. It would be a mistake nonetheless to attribute the inculcation of racial logics solely to the German occupation. In addition to creating administrative hurdles in everyday life, the fixing of nationality in Soviet identity documents provided a convenient map for the Nazi mass extermination of Jews. No clear plan or directive for a final solution (or the total annihilation of Jews) had been outlined. But in the first months of the war, Nazi Germans, with the help of local collaborators, rounded up Jews in ghettos and concentration camps. Jews were shot in fields or ravines, in a brutal and intimate manner, usually on the outskirts of towns and cities, and buried in mass graves. Soviet administrative records and censuses expedited the mass killing operations. To locate Jews, all German officials needed to do was inspect the paperwork assembled by the vast Soviet bureaucracy. Soviet documentary records—from passports and student identity cards to school rosters, censuses, and job application forms—listed the nationality of every person.[58]

In the borderlands, populations came to view themselves and those around them largely through the prism of race. Mass killing permanently altered the ethnographic order. All groups were demarcated by racial categories or visibly distinct markers. Badges and armbands allowed Nazis to differentiate the "Aryan types" from the "barbaric" Slavs and "subhuman" Jews. Ukrainians wore yellow and blue armbands, while Jews wore white bands or the Star of David. The thousands of ethnic Germans who had resided in Right Bank Ukraine wore distinguishing badges, as well. Nazi officials required everyone over the age of eighteen to carry identification papers with their racial or ethnic identities clearly marked. A wrong identity card could serve as a death sentence. But in the protean borderland—where it was often difficult to differentiate people by language and appearance— identification papers could also save lives.[59] Lev Yurovsky recalled that he had managed to survive the war because of the generosity of his neighbor who had offered him her husband's passport. Yurovsky subsequently put the document "in order" by doctoring the descriptive data, which allowed him to pass as an ethnic Russian man. Other Jews exchanged their Soviet passports for German documents "without the slightest pang of conscience," in hopes that they and their children could evade detection.[60]

The war left a long trail of misery and deprivation. The Soviet Union was subjected to immense material and human loss. Some 27 million people perished during the war, with the male population accounting for 77 percent, or 20 million, deaths. The violence wreaked havoc on Jewish communities, with Jewish deaths totaling approximately 10 percent, or 2.7 million, of all casualties. As the war progressed, the Soviet economy suffered a near total collapse. In places with heavy combat damage, it was often difficult to find shelter. Nearly 70,000 villages and 1,700 towns were destroyed; some 32,000 factories and 40,000 miles of rail track lay in complete ruins; food and consumer-good supply incurred drastic cuts. The postwar economic recovery, with respect to food, housing, and manufacturing of consumer goods, was unusually long and painful. The Soviet Union reached the prewar gross national production level only in 1948.[61]

At war's end, amid chaos and confusion, Jewish survivors found themselves in hostile circumstances. In western Belarus and western Ukraine, Nazi Germans took considerable efforts to confiscate Jewish property: money, clothing, furniture, housing, and valuables such as silver, gold, and jewelry. Household and personal items were used by the German administration, redistributed among ethnic Germans, turned over to local policemen or collaborators, or pawned off to eager neighbors. In the post-occupation months, with housing and material belongings in short supply, property conflicts were the norm of the day. In a country devastated by total war, many survivors had no homes or apartments to return to. Others found their prewar apartments inhabited by non-Jewish acquaintances or discovered that their furniture, clothing, kitchen items, and other material belongings were in possession of a former neighbor. Resolving disputes or tracing how property changed hands was no easy task. It was not unusual for Jews to encounter violence or hostilities when they tried to recover private possessions. If all else failed, Jews could petition party leaders or turn to local courts to seek justice, but in most cases, turning to Soviet authorities for the restitution of property proved unsuccessful.[62]

Postwar rage hampered reconstruction. Long before Soviet authorities began to harass and arrest prominent Jewish cultural figures and medical experts in 1948, culminating in the infamous Doctor's Plot in 1953, anti-Semitism created obstacles for Jews in their everyday life. Emil Draitser, who grew up in Odessa, remembered how shameful he felt when his teacher mispronounced his name in front of the class. In the fall of 1945, on the first day of school, school children made fun of the boy because the name "Draitser" did not sound Russian, and, instead, called him a little kike and a Jew.[63] Mary Leder, an American teenager from Santa Monica, California, who emigrated with her parents to Birobidzhan and then went on to live in the Soviet Union for some thirty-four years, recalled that drunks called Jews *zhidy* on the streets, and Jewish children were taunted in the courtyard. Anti-Semitic remarks and accusations "became commonplace in the long lines to buy food," according to Leder. Soviet authorities did not try to curb the outbursts. "Whereas before the war, anyone who ventured to utter a racial or ethnic slur in public could be hauled before a court of law and punished, it would be a foolish person indeed who tried to take a tormenter to court now."[64]

In the months following the war, the situation became alarming on many levels, with Jews beset by widespread rumors, threats, and insults. Stalin's paranoid attack on the loyalty of Jewish subjects and the anti-cosmopolitan campaign played out on the front pages of leading Soviet newspapers, creating an atmosphere of intimidation and fear. Jews were depicted as an eternal alien and singled out for unreliability and unworthiness. Soviet publications referred to Jews as "poor and rotten soldiers."[65]

Olga Freidenberg, a professor of classical philology in Leningrad, observed that educated people with recognizably Jewish names were subjected to "moral lynching." "One could see the pogrom as carried out in our department. Groups of students rummage through the works of Jewish professors, eavesdrop on private conversations, whisper in corners. They make no effort to conceal their purposeful vigilance."[66] In March 1953, the prominent film director, M. I. Romm, complained directly to Stalin that he was forced to recall his ethnic origins frequently, even though he (like so many other Soviet Jews) was raised in Moscow, spoke only Russian, and had always felt completely Russian.[67]

Unofficial quotas for Jewish students in law, medicine, and culture and the arts added to the daily frustrations. Finding gainful employment proved particularly trying. The internal passport—with the word "Jew" (Evrei) on the fifth line—did not help matters. After failing to land a job, one survivor recalled:

> I never hid that I was a Jew. Why hide it? It's not a source of pride, but still. I, so to say, have suffered quite a bit because I was a Jew.

You couldn't get a job if you were a Jew. For me it was harder than it was for my father. My father witnessed limitations before the revolution. He would say, "You passed by a store, and there was a sign in the window: 'Jews not welcome here.'" It was easier [under the Tsarist regime]. In our times, you come, you see "Wanted," and they don't hire you. And sometimes they even tell you the reason they don't hire you.

"For nine months," a recent graduate noted, "I walked from one bank to another. I would call them and ask, 'Do you hire graduates of the [Moscow Geological Institute]? They would say, 'Yes. Our institute ranks very well.' They would tell me to come in. I'd go in. They'd open my passport, and say, 'You know, we've already hired someone.'"[68]

Soviet anti-Semitism, despite making daily life astonishingly difficult for Jews, did not publicly justify racial discrimination or go to the self-conscious extreme of drawing exclusionary lines. Unlike the United States government, for instance, the Soviet regime did

Image 3.4 A typical internal passport of a Soviet citizen. The nationality is listed as Jewish on the fifth line. © Courtesy of Alexander Frenkel.

not regulate familial relations or interethnic marriage according to a one-drop rule, nor was it concerned with maintaining neat divisions between people who married out of their nationalities. On the contrary, Soviet law viewed mixed marriage as a natural form of social relations. Mixed familial unions, at least officially, strengthened the "friendship of the peoples" principle: a metaphor for anti-racism and proletarian unity of an imagined multiethnic brotherhood. "In our country every sixth family includes people of different nationalities," one Soviet expert proudly declared. "This is one of the clear manifestations of friendly international relations established in the country during the period of Soviet power."[69]

At a time when the American legal system championed interracial marriage as unnatural and immoral, Soviet civil marriage law allowed populations to marry whomever they wished. With more than 100 different nationalities residing within the borders of the Soviet Union, mixed families came in many different combinations.[70] Jews intermarried at particularly high rates, with the frequency increasing over the course of the Soviet century. In 1936, around 13 percent of Jews in Belarus chose to marry non-Jewish spouses. The numbers were slightly higher in Ukraine at 15 percent and expanded in Russia to 40 percent. After World War II the rates ballooned even higher. By the time the Soviet Union collapsed, around 60 percent of all males and around 50 percent of all females were married to non-Jewish spouses, with the proportion highest in Moscow and Leningrad.[71]

Mixed unions unsettled the categories of Russianness and Jewishness. Official attitudes toward mixed unions remained welcoming, even celebratory, but intermarried couples and their partially Jewish children found it difficult to free themselves of the burdens of their origins. It was not uncommon for mixed Jewish families and children to encounter disparaging comments, including ethnic slurs. Parents and children faced ridicule because they looked Jewish or bore Jewish-sounding surnames. Commenting on the postwar era, Mary Leder noted that Soviet citizens identified Jews by their names, patronymics, and even by their looks. "It always amazed me," Leder wrote in her memoirs, "how Russians managed to spot as Jews individuals who did not look at all Jewish to me."[72]

Race and Cold War Politics

At the same time that anti-Semitism made Jewish life difficult within Soviet Russia, the regime emerged from World War II as a powerful critic of race relations, particularly of its Cold War rival, the US. From 1946 through the mid-1960s, the Soviet Union renewed its focus in cultivating a carefully constructed image of moral racial superiority. Journalists, graphic artists, and radio broadcasters drew on a repertoire of propaganda tools developed in the interwar period. Propagandists made extensive use of American press coverage, often in graphic detail—including newspaper stories, cartoons, and photographs. In condemning everything from lynchings, beatings, and senseless murders of young Black men by white mobs to racial segregation, economic inequality, and civil rights protests, Soviet propaganda exposed America's hypocrisy as the leader of the "free world," driving home the message that racial violence was symptomatic of the American capitalist system.[73]

As the international drama heated up, public opinion took notice. "The entire world is watching America and the way it handles its racial and religious minorities," the Broadway actor Robert Massey addressed a luncheon at the Waldorf-Astoria Hotel in New York in April 1946. "It matters very much now what the rest of the world thinks of America's treatment of its races."[74] The US federal government was particularly sensitive to international criticism of its treatment of ethnic minorities. President Harry S. Truman (1945–53) adopted a moderate pro-civil rights stance, in hopes of promoting democracy, containing the threat of communism, and maintaining public diplomacy efforts.

America's deeply concerning record on race provided the international community with a trove of sensational material. Soviet newspapers utilized photographs with great effectiveness, as a window onto the troubling experiences of US race relations. They publicized misfortunes of racial violence and discrimination by running shocking, often sarcastic, headlines such as "Racist Orgy for Export," "Bloody Drama in Los Angeles," and "The Tragedy of Colored America."[75] On the question of race prejudice, the Soviet newspaper *Trud* (Labor) observed that "semi-slave forms of oppression and exploitation are

Image 3.5 Soviet anti-racist cartoon, drawing by Victor Efimov, 1978. The building sign reads "Restaurant." A Black boy nails the sign "Whites Only" to the wall, as two white American men stand in the background. © Courtesy of Ne Boltai!

the rule" and that the movement of social equality has resulted in "unbridled terror against the negroes," while *Pravda* (Truth) reported of vicious "pogroms" directed at the Black American community.[76]

US officials felt that the Soviet Union's propaganda efforts routinely disseminated troublesome episodes of domestic civil rights abuse, which damaged the image of American democracy and fueled international outrage. In 1949, the US embassy in Moscow declared that the "Soviet press hammers away unceasingly on such things as 'lynch law,' segregation, racial discrimination, deprivation of political rights, etc., seeking to build up a picture of an America in which the Negroes are brutally downtrodden with no hope of improving their status under the existing form of government." In 1957, when Governor Orval Faubus ordered national troops to block nine African American students from enrolling at Little Rock's Central High School, *Izvestiia* (News) characterized the episode in Arkansas a "tragedy," which aroused "ire and indignation in the heart of every honest man." In southern states such as Arkansas

fascist thugs of the Ku Klux Klan are organizing a savage hunt for Negro children because the latter plan to sit in the same classrooms with white boys and girls. National guard soldiers and policemen armed to the teeth bar Negro children from entering the schools, threaten them with bayonets and tear-gas bombs and encourage hooligans to engage in violence with impunity.[77]

By the early 1960s, according to Thomas Hughes, the assistant secretary of state for US intelligence and research, Soviet broadcasting on race relations in America had grown to "enormous" proportions. In a two-week period in May 1963, the number of Soviet radio broadcasts and newspaper commentaries devoted to US racism grew to seven times the coverage of the Ole Miss riot of 1962 (when segregationists protested the enrollment of James Meredith on the campus); nine times greater than the freedom riders (when civil rights activists rode buses on the interstate in the Deep South in 1961); and more than eleven times the Little Rock Crisis of 1957. In a classified memo, Hughes wrote that America's "racial crisis provides wonderful grist for a propaganda mill which is constantly ready to exploit and publicize any weakness in western society. The greater intensity of the present crisis may account in large part for the expanded Soviet coverage." Unsurprisingly, America's policies toward people of color had troubling implications for international relations. Soviet broadcasters posed the question: If American public officials "can act like slaveholders towards millions of their own people, what can the nations of Asia, Africa, and Latin America expect of them?"[78]

Anti-communist rhetoric dominated the US political airways, while the blunt criticism of Soviet sympathizers threatened US prestige abroad. Civil rights activists such as Du Bois found themselves marginalized for their pro-communist views and censure of US foreign policy. In the last three decades of his life, Du Bois's travels around the world took him from Berlin, Moscow, and Warsaw to Shanghai, Nagasaki, and Cape Town. By drawing connections between racial politics in America and the cruel forces of imperialism around the world, Du Bois reconceptualized racism as a global phenomenon.[79]

While visiting Nazi Germany on an Oberlaender Fellowship in the summer of 1936, Du Bois became acutely aware that Germany's anti-Semitism not only mirrored American color prejudice, but "surpassed in vindictive cruelty and public insult anything" that he had ever witnessed.[80] The events surrounding World War II and the atrocities perpetrated by the Nazis on Jews played a fundamental role in helping Du Bois rethink the unequal treatment of African Americans. Several decades later, lecturing on the destruction of Jews in the Warsaw ghetto at the Hotel Diplomat in New York, Du Bois reflected on the genealogy of his thought process. For Du Bois, the Negro problem was no longer a "matter of color and physical and racial characteristics." "No, the race problem in which I was interested," Du Bois observed, "cut across lines of color and physique and belief and status and was a matter of cultural patterns, perverted teaching and human hate and prejudice, which reached all sorts of people and caused endless evil to all men."[81]

In light of his unwavering commitment to social justice and opposition to racial discrimination, Du Bois continued to ally himself with the Soviet political project. In the fall of 1936, the civil rights activist hoped to make a second extended trip to the USSR to undertake a study of ethnic minorities. To his surprise, the Soviets rejected the visa application, allowing Du Bois to transit in Moscow for only a few days, en route to China and Japan. Du Bois wound up spending most of his time in the USSR in a first-class sleeping car aboard the Trans-Siberian "Lux Express," traveling approximately ten thousand kilometers through six time zones.

In the summer of 1949, Du Bois went to the Soviet Union a third time to participate in the Peace Congress in Moscow. This time, the Soviet press devoted outsized attention to the trip. In the 1950s, Du Bois's star began to rise. Articles by and about Du Bois were published in Soviet newspapers and magazines, while his books and speeches appeared in Russian translation. As his thoughts shifted from Black politics in America to the anti-imperialism of the Pan-African Movement and to the reimagining of racism as an international human rights issue, Soviet Russia continued to occupy a special place in Du Bois's conception of the global color line. In no other modern land, Du Bois asserted in *Russia and America*, had he witnessed "so little consciousness of racial differences as in Russia today." Although Du Bois had no illusion that Soviet Russia was an anti-racist utopia, he was impressed nonetheless by its integrationist policies. "Every effort is evidently being made to make the artisan and handworkers the social equal of the [white-collar] worker, the professional man, the teacher, the civil servant."[82] Elsewhere, he described the Soviet Union as "the most hopeful nation on earth."[83]

His contemporaries described Du Bois as an enemy of the state for making "hate-America speeches." The publisher Harcourt, Brace, and Company declined to publish *Russia and America* because the book failed to provide "a balanced interpretation" and, furthermore, appeared to be "an uncritical apologia for Soviet Russia and an excessive condemnation of the United States." Meanwhile, the US passport office repeatedly denied the political pariah permission to travel overseas for refusing to fill out a questionnaire detailing his ties to the Communist Party. Du Bois's FBI file grew to a hefty tome, encompassing everything from newspaper clippings, pamphlets, personal correspondence to passport application files, detailed summaries of overseas speeches, and radio broadcasts.[84]

Despite the unwelcome public scrutiny, Du Bois's commitment to the Soviet project remained unwavering. In 1958, on the heels of a landmark Supreme Court decision that reinstated his passport, the elderly Du Bois went on an eleven-month sojourn across the Atlantic, with stops in England, Holland, France, Czechoslovakia, East Germany, the Soviet Union, and China. The Soviet press heralded Du Bois as an international symbol of peace activism. Soviet journalists photographed him at red-carpet receptions; at a New Year's party at the Kremlin; at an honorary degree ceremony at Moscow State University; conversing side by side with Nikita Khrushchev (1953–64) in the Kremlin; and at the African and Asian Writers Conference in Tashkent, where delegates greeted the appearance of the "90-year-old globe trotter," the father of modern pan-Africanism, with "wild

Image 3.6 W. E. B. Du Bois and Nikita Khrushchev at a conference in the Kremlin, November 7, 1958. W. E. B. Du Bois Papers (MS 312). © Courtesy of Special Collections and University Archives, University of Massachusetts Amherst Libraries.

Image 3.7 W. E. B. Du Bois and Shirley Graham Du Bois with two unidentified children viewing the May Day parade in a large crowd in Moscow's Red Square, May 1, 1959. W. E. B. Du Bois Papers (MS 312). © Courtesy of Special Collections and University Archives, University of Massachusetts Amherst Libraries.

applause and cheers."[85] Du Bois's highly anticipated meeting with Khrushchev played an instrumental role in the creation of the Pan-African Institute within the Soviet Academy of Sciences. On his return to the US, Du Bois received the 1958 International Lenin Peace Prize at a special ceremony at the Soviet Embassy in Washington

D.C., in recognition of his "outstanding service in the struggle for the preservation and strengthening of peace in the whole world."[86]

As the Cold War crisis lingered on, Soviet propagandists touted the modern technological achievements of the Soviet state, its progressive anti-racist politics and commitment to anti-colonial struggles. Under Khrushchev's leadership, the Kremlin's approach to Third World alliances softened. With censorship standards relaxed, the Soviet Union committed considerable resources to subsidizing literary and cultural production, including the translation and publication of foreign literatures and the hosting of film festivals, literary conferences, and youth festivals, aimed at showcasing its commitment to non-whiteness.[87] To develop closer relations with the developing world, the Soviet regime provided political and military support, generous loans and scholarships, and mass technical and professional training to students from Africa, Asia, and Latin America. In 1961, some 500 African students studied in the USSR at the Lumumba University or "Friendship University," which catered to third world students. By 1989, around 36,000 students from Sub-Saharan Africa and nearly 39,600 students from Latin America graduated from Soviet institutions of higher education and technical schools. The plan was for students from the Third World to "become not only highly qualified specialists but also persons with progressive opinion, true friends of the Soviet Union," according to a secret decree issued by the Central Committee of the Communist Party.[88]

Third World students arrived in the Soviet Union expecting a mecca, but as Jan Carew described in *Green Winter*, an autobiographical novel about a Black student from Guyana, they found no angels. Much like their counterparts in the United States, foreign students studying in the Soviet Union encountered race discrimination, verbal sneers, racial profiling, and occasionally physical abuse. In Moscow, four Russian students beat up a Somali student for dancing with a white Russian girl, while another Russian girl was expelled from university for a romantic relationship with an African student. A female graduate student from Leningrad State University recalled that Russian women developed romantic relationships with foreign students largely for pragmatic reasons (because foreigners had more money or were

Image 3.8 In 1955 and 1956, the Everyman Opera Company staged fourteen performances in Leningrad of the famed American opera *Porgy and Bess*, followed by twelve performances in Moscow, with the Soviet Ministry of Culture paying the tour costs in full. The US State Department sponsored overseas tours of US musicians and dancers, as well as cultural presentations as "ambassadors of the arts." But in 1953 and on several occasions thereafter, it declared that a production of *Porgy and Bess* in the Soviet Union would be "politically premature." The Soviet Ministry of Culture paid $16,000 a week ($141,000 in 2014), in addition to transportation costs, food and lodging in the Hotel Astoria and the Hotel Metropol, as well as excursions around the capital cities, entertainment, and large holiday banquets. The production of *Porgy and Bess* received outsized international attention, with journalists and photographers from major US newspapers and magazines covering the premieres and Nikita Khrushchev and other political dignitaries in attendance. © Courtesy of Manuel Litran/Paris Match via Getty Images.

perceived as intellectual and well mannered), which triggered feelings of insecurity and hostility among (white) Soviet men.[89]

Similar incidents of name-calling and harassment played out in many other cities in the USSR. African students were called "black monkeys" and "idlers" and were taunted to wash their "black bodies." Emboldened by anti-racist struggles in the international sphere and the rhetoric of postcolonial liberation, African students protested racist mistreatment, squalid sanitary conditions, and tacit restrictions on socializing and dating Russian girls. In a scathing editorial, African students who were expelled from Moscow State University for participating in a Black African Student Union had no qualms calling out the Soviet Union's anti-racist, color-blind posturing: "For the Soviet leaders to pose before the world as champions of oppressed Africa while they oppress millions in their own country and their satellites is hypocrisy at its worst."[90]

Soviet authorities did their best to keep the reports of mistreatment and abuse under wraps, preserving the carefully crafted image of moral racial superiority. In most cases, the incidents did not make for sensational international headlines. On rare occasions, however, an alleged hate crime—a grisly murder of an African student—generated international news coverage. Soviet authorities dismissed the death as an unfortunate outcome of "alcohol-induced stupor," but African students countered that it was a racially induced crime, a matter of "white against black." On December 19, 1963, some 500 to 700 African students enrolled in Soviet universities and technical institutes walked in the center of the capital, shouting "Moscow, a second Alabama" and "Stop Killing Africans!" The event received outsized attention in the media, causing Soviet officials to confront a foreign relations nightmare.[91]

Blackness—a marker of foreignness and exoticism, if not alienation—increasingly occupied a conspicuous place in Soviet society. Students from Somalia, Ghana, and Kenya were not the only ones who encountered racist taunts, jokes, and profiling in their daily life. In the 1960s and 1970s, tens of thousands of Soviet citizens from the Caucasus and Central Asia traveled long distances to Moscow and Leningrad in search of new educational and economic opportunities.

Tatars, Georgians, Azerbaijanis, Kyrgyz, and Tajiks left small towns and villages for the Soviet capitals hoping to improve their social standing. The lucky few studied in institutions of higher education and technical schools; a handful landed coveted white-collar jobs. Most dark-skinned newcomers from the southern republics and eastern peripheries occupied liminal spaces in the capital cities, without right of residence or access to health care and education. The migrants earned modest salaries in service and construction sectors and sold their wares on street corners and at bus and metro stations, where they were often called "black monkeys," "*negry*," "black snouts," and a litany of other racially insensitive insults ascribed to their hair or skin color.[92]

In the last years of his life, Du Bois continued to praise Soviet Russia for her "refusal to be white"—for "not lining up against the colored peoples of the world" and "increasing long smoldering resentment."[93] Soviet law supported the upbeat assessment. The Bolshevik state provided its citizens equal protection and treatment, regardless of ethnic origins. It was also the only superpower that spread its anti-colonial and anti-racist message internationally to the Afro-Asian world. But by the time the USSR collapsed, Soviet internationalism had lost much of its global appeal, while, at home, the boundaries between Russians and dark-skinned populations began to harden. People who identified themselves as "Russian" became increasingly conscious of the outsized role that skin color played in elevating their place as the first among equals in Soviet society. This development, it turned out, not only had long-term implications for forging intimate bonds between Russianness and whiteness, but for everyday ethnic relations as well, which took an increasingly sinister turn in the 1990s and beyond.

CHAPTER 4
WHITE RAGE

Russia's post-Soviet transition resulted in poverty, pain, and a shared sense of loss. Unchecked inflation and food shortages caused most Russians to feel that the country was descending into chaos and anarchy. People lined up for forty to sixty-eight hours per month on average to purchase basic foodstuffs. By April 1991, meat and butter rarely showed up in stores; when they did, prices surged by 300 percent or more. The rest of the decade proved no better. Currency devaluations, culminating in the 1998 market crash, and a staggering 13.2 percent unemployment rate (between 1994 and 1998), added to the perception that relative stability had become a thing of the past. In the anemic economic climate of the 1990s, even as living standards stabilized, most people fell below the poverty line at least once. As Russia's unofficial economy and retail trade took off, so did the unequal distribution of income. In 1997, the ten richest Russians controlled 3.5 percent of the country's GDP, but the poverty rate nearly doubled as a result of the 1998 financial crisis.[1]

No less troubling was Russia's mortality crisis. No other industrialized nation at peace experienced such a steep loss in population, which declined by roughly two million in eight years (from 148.5 in 1992 to 146.5 in 2000). A combination of factors, including excessive alcohol consumption, drug dependency, and a rise in psychological stress and suicide resulted in the sharp drop. By the beginning of the twenty-first century, Russia's suicide rate spiked to its highest in many decades; the fertility rate plunged to among the lowest in the world. The rise in mortality, especially among middle-aged ethnic Russian men, the population that suffered the most, heightened personal vulnerability, contributing to the uncertainties in everyday life. In 1993, life expectancy for males dropped below sixty years, and remained at that level for many years thereafter. In 1994, a twenty-year-old Russian male had only a one in two chance of surviving to age sixty; the death rate of working-age males was approximately four times that of US males.[2]

In all, the recovery rates were so slow that experts predicted that the population decline would continue for decades to come. At the turn of the new millennium, some demographers spoke of "an unprecedented pace of deterioration in a country not at war."[3] Other public health professionals claimed that Russia had descended into a full-blown demographic crisis, predicting that the country's population would eventually fall to less than 100 million, if policy makers failed to take bold steps to rectify the problem. In his first annual address to the Federal Assembly of the Russian Federation in July 2000, Vladimir Putin characterized the population question as "one of the most alarming that the country faces." "We, the citizens of Russia, are becoming fewer and fewer with each passing year," he remarked. Putin estimated that Russia's population had dropped by an average of 750,000 annually since the collapse of the Soviet Union. If the mortality rates remained constant, the number of Russian citizens would drop by 22 million by 2015. "I would ask you to think this figure over," Putin told his audience. "We really do face the threat of becoming an enfeebled nation."[4]

Adding fuel to the fire was the precipitous decline of the ethnic Russian majority. According to the 2010 census, the number of ethnic Russians (relative to the population as a whole) had fallen from 81.5 percent, or 119.9 million, in 1989, to 77.7 percent, or 111 million, in 2010. The decline of the ethnic Russian majority occurred as the share of non-Russians, especially from the Caucasus and Central Asia, accelerated. For decades, Soviet social scientists charted the discrepancy in the birth rates among ageing Slavs in the heartland and young people from the Caucasus and Central Asia, the poorest of the Soviet republics. Journalists and television commentators picked up on the jarring statistical trends, warning of the social dangers that Tatars, Bashkirs, Chechens, Kabards, Ingush, and a host of other dark-skinned groups such as Avars, Dargins, and Kumyks posed to Russian cultural values.[5]

White Power Violence

Just as Russia was experiencing an epidemic of "deaths of despair," violence—directed at Chechens, Jews, Africans, Central Asians, and Roma—surged.[6] One leading expert claimed that, in the new millennium, Russia had become a racial tinderbox, "the most dangerous country for racist violence in the world."[7] Over the course of eighteen years, between 2000 and 2017, at least 458 people died as a result of extremist crimes and thousands more were beaten or wounded. In the mid-1990s, a diverse right-wing movement came on the scene in cities such as Moscow, Voronezh, Riazan, Tiumen, Rostov-on-Don, and St. Petersburg. By 2007, Russia was home to some 60,000 to 65,000 skinheads. Armed with weapons and explosives, militant gangs such as Combat-18, the Nationalist Socialist Society, the Brotherhood of Skins, the Slavic Union, and the Aryan Brotherhood identified themselves as defenders of the great white race. White power extremists organized training camps and knife-fighting sessions, with the explicit goal of preserving the white Russian nation from foreigners and dark-skinned minorities.[8]

It is hard to provide an overarching explanation for the upsurge of racial violence and xenophobic attitudes. A multiplicity of factors— the uneven state of the economic recovery, including Russia's own "deaths of despair," a lack of confidence in Putin's policies, as well as anxieties over the influx of migrant populations from the southern border—set the stage for racial strife.[9] White power extremists capitalized on Russia's social and political upheavals to recruit new members, relying on the internet to spread their message and to publish videos of violent exploits and paramilitary training sessions. They livestreamed grisly attacks, masterminded misinformation campaigns, and shared racist memes, video clips, propaganda, and manuals. More than 100 newspapers and at least seven publishing houses peddled extremist views. White power militants organized robust rallies to spread their message to the public, most famously on National Unity Day (commemorated on November 4, beginning in 2005). But it was the online spaces, including fringe social-media websites and digital platforms, that allowed right-wing militancy to thrive. Over 800 websites openly promoted hate crimes, cultivated new members, spurred right-wing activism, and spread conspiracy theories, far-right disinformation campaigns, and hateful rhetoric.[10]

White power violence played out in a tumultuous social and political context of post-Soviet Russia, but it always spoke to larger global historical forces, events, and ideas. Participating in a global culture of hate, right-wing extremists expressed exclusionary fantasies rooted in the superiority of whiteness. The slogan "white power," in Russia and elsewhere around the world, served as the rallying cry. Some militants wore tactical boots, shaved their heads, and tattooed their bodies with neo-pagan symbols; many others grew their hair and looked like other "hard-working, kind-hearted kids."[11] Activists played on societal fears by claiming that dark-skinned migrants posed a demographic threat to the white Russian majority. "The Russian people are dying; we are being degraded by other races. It's time for someone to say enough,

Image 4.1 Extremist-nationalists, shouting "Russia for the Russians," "Moscow for the Muscovites," and other white power slogans, marching on Unity Day in the southeastern outskirts of Moscow on November 4, 2013. About 10,000 Russian nationalists gathered across Moscow in an annual show of anger against the presence of Muslim migrants. © Courtesy of Vasily Maximov/AFP via Getty Images.

and for us to stand and fight," Dmitry Diumushkin, the founder of the extreme nationalist group Slavic Union, proclaimed.[12]

In a world filled with alcohol, drugs, and laundered money, white power activists typically congregated in high-rise, low-income apartment buildings or abandoned construction projects on the outskirts of cities. But they also hung out in bars such as the Grease Club on Malaia Ordynka Street, decorated wall-to-wall with American confederate flags, only a few blocks from the Tretiakov Gallery in the very center of Moscow.[13] One manifesto summed up the existential threat, affirming that Russia's extremists "are white warriors" or "soldiers of their race and nation," who stand on the front lines of a global racial war, "fighting every day for the future of the white race and the happiness of their people."[14]

A crude, paranoid anti-Semitism resurfaced. Anti-Semitic references appeared regularly in periodicals, magazines, television shows, and newspapers, even though a tiny Jewish community remained in the Russian Federation, with most Jews emigrating to North America and Israel. The Anti-Defamation Committee of the Russian–Jewish Congress classified nearly 200 newspapers as openly anti-Semitic. A pollster for the All-Union Center for the Study of Public Opinion remarked, "The fewer Jews there are in Russia, the more they talk about them." Russian politicians such as the Communist Party leader Gennady Zyuganov blamed the "current catastrophic conditions of the country" on the global conspiracy of Jews, while *Pamiat'* (Memory) and other ultra-nationalist groups embraced conspiratorial thinking, calling for the destruction of Jewish monuments and violence toward Jews. Skinheads vandalized Jewish graveyards, synagogues, and community centers; inscribed swastikas and stars of David on gravestones; and erected anti-Semitic signs such as "Jews, return to your homeland."[15]

Far-right extremism emerged as a powerful social phenomenon. The number of right-wing attacks in Russia was five times more than in the United States and four times more than in Germany and twice more than in Sweden (the two countries with the highest right-wing militancy in Western Europe). Activists committed violence in the name of an all-white ethnic Russian nation. "A skinhead," one extremist member testified in a court of law, "is a person who loves their nation. To affirm our love for the nation, I, together with other skinheads, went to football matches, went to fight with the fans of other football teams, and beat people of non-Slavic appearance."[16]

Discriminatory attitudes on the grounds of race became a fact of life for anyone who did not "look typically ethnic Russian," according to the Amnesty International.[17] The violence took on a number of different forms: from xenophobic slurs to knife attacks, premeditated murders, and full-blown riots, involving hundreds of attackers and causing massive amounts of property damage to shopping centers and outdoor fruit and vegetable markets. On streets, trolleybuses, and subways, skinheads sowed discord: harassing and attacking, often with fatal consequences, Africans, Koreans, Central Asians, Caucasians, Roma, and children of mixed ethnic parentage. "I know that skinheads attack people who do not look Russian, and I am not Russian," an Armenian student recalled. "You can see that in my appearance. I've got dark hair and brown eyes. All nationalities have distinct characteristics such as Armenians, Georgians, or Adygheans. . . . It doesn't matter really, but they only attack non-Russians."[18]

In the new millennium, a wave of grisly hate crimes made for international headlines. Media outlets reported of hundreds of racist attacks on ethnic minorities, with some 800 hate crimes occurring in 2005 alone. In July 2002, at a summer picnic in Moscow, ten Russian men assaulted a group of African students, refugees, and asylum-seekers, shouting "white power" and other racist slogans. The picnickers stopped a police patrol car, but the officer refused to help, claiming that the area was beyond his jurisdiction. When new officers arrived on the scene, instead of filing a report, they accused the picnickers of instigating the attack and proceeded to inspect identity papers, before taking the young men for further questioning to a nearby police station.[19]

In February 2004, in another high-profile case, a gang of teenagers used an assortment of weapons—knuckledusters, chains, sticks, and knives—to attack a Tajik family in the courtyard of an apartment building. Shouting "Russia for the Russians," the gang repeatedly stabbed Khrusheda Sultanova, a nine-year-old girl, and proceeded to beat up her father and her eleven-year-old cousin. Khrusheda died of excessive blood loss. Her father sustained nonthreatening head injuries, while her cousin saved her life by hiding underneath a nearby car. And in April 2006, a member of the right-wing organization Mad Crowd, shouting Nazi slogans, attacked a group of African students in the center of St. Petersburg, on the doorsteps of African Unity, a cultural organization founded with the mission of promoting tolerance and friendship among Russians and foreigners. The attacker shot to death a Senegalese student named Samba Lampsar but managed to run away before the police could apprehend him. The shotgun, decorated with a swastika and the inscription "white power," was found at the scene of the crime.[20]

As right-wing extremism escalated, human rights organizations began to take notice. In June 2006, Doudou Diène, the United Nations special rapporteur on racism, visited Moscow and St. Petersburg on an inspection tour. In his report to the Human Rights Council, Diène observed that "Russian society is facing an alarming trend of racism and xenophobia, the most striking manifestations of which are the increasing number of racially motivated crimes and attacks, including by neo-Nazi groups, particularly against people of non-Slav appearance originating in the Caucasus, Africa, Asia, or the Arab world." All sorts of people, from different regions of the Russian Federation, were drawn to the mass movement. "The average skinhead profile is no longer that of a socially disadvantaged and uneducated youth," Diène declared, "but rather a teenager—increasingly often a minor—from a middle-class family with secondary, higher, or technical education." In most cases, members were in their teens or early twenties, with girls and young women participating in the violence, as well.[21]

White power groups such as the National Socialist Society advocated revolutionary terrorism not only to sow discord—although they did that and more—but to create an opposition movement to destabilize the very foundations of the state. In this respect, there was nothing particularly unusual in the ideas and attributes that shaped extremist violence in the New Russia. White power activists from America to Germany and Australia saw the state largely in adversarial terms. "We realized that we're living in an occupied state—that our homeland is currently in enemy hands," one Russian extremist explained. "The regime of Putin, the chekists, and the FSB has seized power, and those who speak out against them are locked away in prison and killed."[22]

Moscow looked to the white power movement as a potentially useful tool for galvanizing support among its base of supporters. Law enforcement agencies often turned a blind eye to extremist violence—particularly when it came to attacks against dark-skinned minorities. But Putin drew a red line when far-right mobilization infringed on the power of the state. The Kremlin expressed no tolerance for extremist violence that undermined or destabilized the state's governing structures.

Still, there is little doubt that Putin's authoritarian politics made it possible for white militarism to flourish. Putin's administration not only supported the European Far Right—by most famously underwriting the activities of the Front National in France—but also provided a model for white nationalist rule all around the world.[23] "Putin has said that everyone should feel at home here, and that is of course welcome [sic]," proclaimed Petr Indogeno, the general secretary of African Students at the Russian University of Peoples' Friendship of Russia, "But we want to feel safe, not at home."[24] The ideological vacuum left by the collapse of the Soviet Union created what Diène described as a "cocktail," or a "culture favorable to the emergence of groups of individuals and of political parties that have used the racist and xenophobic platform as its main discourse."[25] Amnesty International and other human rights organizations have repeatedly characterized Moscow's response to racism as "grossly inadequate."[26] The Ministry of Justice and the Supreme Court may have prohibited the registration of organizations with extremist platforms, including, in a 2005 landmark decision, Rodina, the fourth largest political party. Authorities may have convicted several high-profile groups of hate crimes. But by routinely classifying xenophobic attacks as "hooliganism"—a petty crime payable by a small fine—rather than as racially motivated hate crimes, the legal system helped fuel racism, while law enforcement officers routinely ignored or covered up racial discrimination, particularly when directed at dark-skinned populations from the southern border.

The Southern Border

After the disintegration of the Soviet Union, Yeltsin and other government officials were reluctant to define the Russian Federation exclusively in ethnic Russian terms, and continued to refer to Russia as a multicultural and multireligious entity. By law, Russian citizenship did not depend on ethnicity or language but on civic loyalty. Nonethnic Russians represented around 20 percent of the population. Ukrainians and Belarusians—considered fellow Slavs by temperament, appearance, and civilization—formed significant minorities, while the Finno-Ugric populations and the peoples of Siberia and the Far North spoke mostly Russian, practiced a form of Eastern Orthodoxy, and did not differentiate themselves all that much from ethnic Russians. The biggest threat to Russian cultural dominance came from the southern border: the traditionally Muslim populations from the Caucasus and Central Asia whose skin and hair color, physiognomy, language, cultural expressions, and occupations reinforced common perceptions of difference.[27]

When Chechnya, a predominantly Muslim republic, located in an obscure mountainous region of the North Caucasus, declared national independence, the Russian armed forces unleashed unusually destructive attacks. The first war in Chechnya was fought in the name of preserving Russia's territorial integrity. In no uncertain terms, the military maneuvers, between 1994 and 1996, were considered an abject failure, resulting in an abrupt cease-fire and the demoralization of Russian troops. The second war in Chechnya, beginning in September 1999, played a central role in the consolidation of Putin's political power.

Putin did his best to avoid Yeltsin's follies. Putin's political legitimacy rested, in large part, on restoring Russia's vigor. When a series of explosions destroyed apartment buildings in Moscow, causing widespread panic, he calmed the public, famously declaring in September 1999, "We will go after them [i.e., gangs of foreign mercenaries and terrorists, or Chechens and other dark-skinned peoples from the Caucasus], wherever they are. If, pardon me, we find them in the toilet, we will waste them in the outhouse."[28] Between his assuming power in 2000 and his reelection to a third presidential term in 2012 and beyond, Putin remade Russia squarely in the image of an all-dominant white male. Showcasing youth and machismo, Putin supported rebuilding a strong centralized state, vowing to protect the population from domestic terrorism and political anarchy. He paid lip service to Russia's multiethnic and multireligious heritage—to the antiquated "friendship of people" metaphor—and elevated ethnic Russianness to the dominant status.

Purposefully avoiding the terms "ethnic conflict" and "racial war," Putin framed the Chechen campaign as an anti-terrorist operation, fought against well-trained international saboteurs who undermined Russia's national security. In an address to the Parliamentary Assembly of the Council of Europe in 2001, the foreign minister, Igor Ivanov, declared that nationalism does not exist in Russia, a multinational state. "Any isolated manifestations of unwelcome nationalism that occur are dealt with appropriately. In no way do we consider the conflict to be interethnic or religious."[29]

The second war in Chechnya caused some 75,000 civilian deaths, although the precise figure is impossible to determine with certainty (the Russian government banned journalists and human rights monitors from traveling to the region). Grozny, the capital of Chechnya, suffered extensive damage to its infrastructure, including to telephone, electricity, and gas lines, water reservoirs, bridges and roads, and the airport. Russian armed forces committed extensive human rights abuses. Sweep operations terrorized civilians, resulting in summary executions, including sexual violence toward Chechen women. Torture—mock executions, electric shock, and genital beatings—turned into official state policy, encouraged by military leaders not only to gather sensitive information but also to humiliate the victims.

As the armed forces left Grozny and surrounding towns and villages in ruins, Moscow conducted a particularly virulent propaganda campaign. Television broadcasts and newspaper articles labeled Chechens as international terrorists, the lowest form of humanity. In popular and military language, racial prejudice easily mixed with anti-terrorist ideology to justify the extreme violence. Referring to

Chechens as "apes," "bandits," and "blacks," soldiers exerted force with impunity. Some 250,000 displaced Chechen civilians fled the war zone. Most went by car, trucks, or on foot to the neighboring republic of Ingushetia, others traveled longer distances to Georgia, Azerbaijan, and Turkey, and a steady stream of migrants departed the economically depressed region for Moscow and other cities in the heartland of the Russian Federation.

Determined to keep Chechens in their place, military leaders sought to control the mass exodus of displaced persons. The Russian government refused to grant Chechen civilians the status of internally displaced persons through the Federal Law on Forced Migrants, which meant, among other things, that forced migrants did not have access to health care, employment, or the right to establish residence in cities and towns in the Russian Federation outside their place of origin. Some politicians such as Yuri Luzhkov, the mayor of Moscow, hoped that a concrete barrier around Chechnya, similar to the Berlin Wall, would protect Russians from terrorists.[30]

A "wall of separation" around Chechnya never got built. But a messy and overly bureaucratic system of migration controls expedited the harassment of ethnic minorities. After the collapse of the Soviet Union, Moscow abolished the notorious passport-*propiska* system. Article 27 of the 1993 Russian Federation Constitution guaranteed people the right to move around the country and to choose a place of residence, either on a permanent or temporary basis, while the internal passport, a required document, no longer bore the holder's ethnicity. But even as Moscow liberalized the laws on mobility, it displayed little tolerance for integrating non-Slavic populations. The policy of visa-free entry, on a ninety-day limit, made it easy for citizens of the Commonwealth of Independent Post-Soviet states (CIS) to cross the sprawling Russian border. The system, however, did not provide work authorization, and the highly cumbersome bureaucratic procedures wound up creating disincentives for employers to comply with the letter of the law.[31]

Between 1992 and 2006, more than 11 million people migrated to the Russian Federation from post-Soviet states—with the share of ethnic Russians steadily declining over the years. By the turn of

Image 4.2 A photograph taken on October 25, 2013, showing migrant workers in a fenced holding area outside Moscow's Federal Migration Service office, waiting to receive a work permit. © Courtesy of Vasily Maximov/AFP via Getty Images.

the twenty-first century, an estimated 4.5 million undocumented migrants (mostly from Central Asia and the Caucasus) resided in Russia proper. The presence of dark-skinned populations from the southern peripheries—Uzbekistan, Tajikistan, Azerbaijan, Kyrgyzstan, Armenia, Moldova, and other former Soviet republics, as well as the troublesome regions of the North Caucasus (part of the Russian Federation)—altered the urban landscape. As in the last decades of the Soviet Union, this population (often stigmatized as "blacks," or *chernye*, due to their appearance, speech, and behavior) operated at the margins of society.[32]

Members of the dominant Russian society looked at non-Slavic migrants from the peripheries as racial outsiders. Anyone who looked or spoke differently could be labeled as "black." "They see a non-Russian face," one Armenian student from Krasnodar remarked, "and call them either Adyghean or Armenian, whatever suits them. Everyone is lumped together under one nationality." Non-Slavs acquired a lowly status. They concentrated in particular professions and trades. Some individuals, including Roma, worked in construction, road repair, wholesale markets, hotels, and restaurants. Many others drove taxis and buses, cleaned sidewalks and apartment buildings, operated vegetable and fresh fruit stands, and hawked vodka, scarves, and cheap earrings in outdoor bazaars and pedestrian underpasses. One Kelderari Roma welder remarked to an American researcher: "All Russians care about is whether you're black or white . . . we are negry. We are treated like a second class here, like your blacks in America."[33]

The federal laws on mobility—and the enforcement mechanisms—turned increasingly harsher as Putin ramped up the second campaign in Chechnya. Moscow considered migrants—and especially peoples of non-Slavic origin—a burden on the city's resources. In the early 2000s, authorities subjected dark-skinned populations to endless episodes of harassment, most of which had something to do with the laws on movement and residence: arbitrary inspections of documents, including requests for proof of employment; refusal to certify residence registration; denial of medical care; imposition of burdensome fines and fees; and demands for bribes. Random checks of individuals of "non-Slavic appearance" became a common feature of urban life. The statement "They are turning Moscow into a little Caucasus" and other racially charged headlines regularly appeared in the press, calling for the expulsion of undocumented southern migrants.

In his public comments, Putin warned of the destructive consequences of terrorism on Russian soil. "Local conflicts," he reported in a 2006 address to the Federal Assembly, "remain a fertile breeding ground for terrorists, a source of their arms and a field upon which they can test their strength in practice. These conflicts often arise on ethnic grounds, often with inter-religious conflict thrown in, which is artificially fomented and manipulated by extremists of all shades."[34] People from the Caucasus and Central Asia—with no connection to war-torn Chechnya—were targeted disproportionally for abuse. Anyone with a darker appearance could be stopped for a document check. It was not unusual for police officers, in the name of rooting out domestic terrorism, to profile individuals of Caucasian origins as "blacks," particularly at metro or railway stations or in streets and on sidewalks.

Document checks usually resulted in short two-hour detentions—which played out silently, invisibly, unpredictably—but on other occasions, police raids could lead to false drug and weapons charges and mass deportations, attracting widespread attention from journalists and human rights organizations such as the Memorial and the Amnesty International. Between 2010 and 2012, according to data compiled by the Memorial, approximately 90 percent of labor migrants reported that they or someone they knew had been harassed by police authorities. It was not unusual for police officers to confiscate passports, registration papers, and work permits, to take "foreigners" into custody without justification, to torture or insult at will, and to extort bribes. Occasionally, a document check could result in the confiscation of large sums of money and valuables, which is what happened in May 2012, when a police officer detained a citizen of Georgia, Mamuka Ts., at the Vasileostrovskaia metro station in St. Petersburg. It turned out that Mamuka was returning home—and to his bad luck, after having been paid 100,000 RUB for three months' work. The officer not only confiscated Mamuka's money, but also threatened to harm him if he reported the incident.[35]

Similar encounters took place in metro stations, outdoor markets, bus stops, parks, and railway stations. One woman, a mother of four from Chechnya, recalled how two drunk Slavic-looking men called her "*chernaia*" when she came out of the metro station. "I pulled up my sleeve and said: 'look, dumbasses, I am whiter than you.' They continued to insult me, so I took out my pocketknife, inviting them to fight me. Cowards as [racists] often are, they retreated. I picked up my sports bag from the ground and proceeded to the minibus." In Moscow, young male Caucasians or Central Asians below the age of thirty numbered nearly 20 percent of all metro passengers but represented 40 percent of all detainees. "They see from my face that I am not Russian, so they stop me and inquire about my circumstances, what I do here," one student from the North Caucasus observed. Another student commented on the invisible aspects of racial sentiment: "Well, even if there is no visible hatred towards us, there are certain moments, certain places where you can feel that we are clearly not loved here [in St. Petersburg]. These problems do not exist only [where] people study, or do something, like the arts, but on an everyday level, with [the] people that you do not know personally."³⁶

Labor migrants resorted to a number of strategies to avoid ethnic profiling. They limited their movement or spent as little time as possible in public spaces where they could easily be identified. Some altered their appearance or refrained from wearing conspicuous clothing or accessories that drew attention to their ethnic origins. To pass for light-skinned Slavs, women colored their hair or wore European-style clothing, while men put on baseball caps to partially cover their face. Almost all migrants carried small sums of cash in case they were detained for a document check.³⁷

In interviews and public speeches, Putin continued to praise Russia's tolerance of diversity. Fast-paced events, however, shattered the perception that post-Soviet life was a brotherhood of nations— embracing all ethnic groups as equal citizens. Terrorist attacks on the Moscow metro and at the Domodedova airport, in 2010 and 2011, respectively, heightened popular resentment against non-Slavic populations. Television networks threw cold water on the "friendship of peoples" metaphor, while promoting the special status of ethnic Russians as the first among equals, and widely reproducing ethno-racial stereotypes in their coverage of crime and interethnic conflict. On talk shows, politicians such as the ultra-nationalist Vladimir Zhirinovskii labeled Russia's multiethnic ideal a thing of the past, which, he claimed, had been destroyed by Dagestanis, Chechens, and other peoples from the North Caucasus. Dmitry Medvedev (who served as president of the Russian Federation from 2008 to 2012) flamed tensions by comparing Russia's "problems" with North Caucasians to what Europe experienced with migrants from North Africa and the Middle East.³⁸

Russian media, diverting criticism away from the Kremlin, played an outsized role in manufacturing ethnic prejudice. This was particularly the case with respect to an event known as the Sviridov affair—the catalyst of one of the largest demonstrations-cum-ethnic riots in post-Soviet Russia. Shortly after midnight on December 6, 2010, two youth groups (one of which was comprised of ethnic Russians, fans of the football club Spartak, and the other one of migrants from the North Caucasus) got into a street brawl. At some point during the fight, Aslan Cherkesov of Kabardino-Balkaria pulled out a gun and shot Yegor Sviridov in the head with a rubber bullet. The police detained Cherkesov, the primary suspect in the murder case, but released five of the accomplices. Rumors began to circulate on social media that the relatives of the North Caucasians paid a handsome bribe to the officers. The next day hundreds of football fans picketed the district prosecutor's office and proceeded to march in protest on the Leningrad Highway, blocking traffic in both directions.

Four days later, on December 11, what was planned as a peaceful memorial rally morphed into a bloody race riot. The violence took place on Manezhnaia Square, only a stone's throw away from the Kremlin and the Red Square. Officials estimated that 5,000 people took to the streets. Some sources wildly inflated the numbers, claiming that as many 50,000 people had gathered that day—a crowd comprised of journalists and police officers and a motley crew of Spartak fans, right-wing extremists of all stripes, and everyday Russians, chanting "Russia for the Russians, Moscow for the Muscovites." One participant described the demonstration as a "racial war," fought by Slavs against Caucasians to preserve the sanctity of the Russian nation. Others professed that the time for peaceful protest had long passed: "In case of conflict, be the first to attack—better to have three court judges sentence you, than four people carry you away. Talk is useless with animals; a beast only understands force . . . to walk without a knife or a gun is criminal negligence." Walking in the direction of the Lenin Library, a mob of rioters chanted anti-immigrant and anti-police slogans, raised their hands in Nazi salute, and attacked randomly people of "non-Slavic appearance."[39]

The Sviridov affair mobilized group solidarity in unexpected ways. Both Putin and Dmitry Medvedev singled out their support for racist actions. In a highly symbolic gesture, Putin, in his capacity as prime minister, laid a wreath on Sviridov's grave, vowing to enact tougher immigration measures. Medvedev, backtracking his original comments, went even further, claiming that there was nothing wrong with elevating ethnic Russians as the first among equals. After all, Medvedev pointed out, "ethnic Russians are the majority in our country. Russian is the state language. The Russian Orthodox Church is the largest religion in our country." It was these characteristics, Medvedev asserted, that comprised the unique makeup of the Russian character. "This is fine, and we should not be afraid to say this."[40]

In the wake of Sviridov's death, demonstrations followed in cities across the Russian Federation—from St. Petersburg and Novosibirsk to the southern port city of Rostov-on-Don, where protestors shouted, "Rostov is an [ethnic] Russian city." Police authorities, blaming the mayhem in Moscow on "left-radical youth" and the problems arising from the criminal behavior of unintegrated minorities and migrants, minimized the role that racist ideologies played in inciting the violence. Predictably, state-sponsored media downplayed the role of popular racial sentiment, although at least one weekly news program spoke of the "epidemics of inter-ethnic conflicts," before attributing the violence to criminal elements from the North Caucasus.[41]

As the Sviridov event and its aftermath unfolded, it became increasingly clear that the mass demonstrations—and the public affirmation of white consciousness—were not solely the work of right-wing nationalists or a group of disenfranchised maniacs. An express poll taken by a popular radio station in Moscow revealed that 87 percent of the listeners supported the mass demonstrations. Similar polls revealed that an overwhelming majority of Russian citizens expressed support for the demonstrations, while calling for "greater rights" for ethnic Russians.[42] To put it in slightly different terms, the people who took to the streets in December 2010 to voice their displeasure at dark-skinned masses from Russia's southern periphery were part of a broad social movement.

"Slavs Only"

On May 7, 2012, Vladimir Putin stepped outside of a black Mercedes and walked along a bright red carpet and up a swirling marble staircase. As he stepped foot through heavy gilded doors inside the Andreevski Hall of the Grand Kremlin Palace, a crowd of 3,000 guests greeted the straight-faced Putin with warm applause. The guest list at the inauguration ceremony included the nation's top military leaders and cabinet members, alongside the head of the Russian Orthodox Church, Patriarch Kirill, and dignitaries such as Mikhail Gorbachev, Boris Yeltsin's widow, Naina, and Putin's longtime friends, the former Italian prime minister Silvio Berlusconi and former Chancellor of Germany Gerhard Schröder. Putin's rarely seen wife Liudmila made an appearance as well. Placing his hand on a red leather-bound copy of the constitution, Putin swore to respect and protect human and civil rights and freedoms. *The Guardian* declared that Putin assumed his third term as Russian president in an "inauguration fit for a king."[43]

As an extravagant dinner party began, groups of boisterous activists took to Moscow's streets to protest the legitimacy of the election. Riot police in camouflage arrested hundreds of people that evening, including the most visible protest leaders, Boris Nemtsov and Alexei Navalny. Anyone wearing a white ribbon, the symbol of protest adopted by anti-Putin activists, was detained and given an official warning. The specter of mass political mobilization—and the highly unfavorable international press coverage—tarred Putin's carefully constructed image of legitimacy. In the aftermath of the inauguration, the Duma passed a whirlwind of restrictive laws to help deflate mass protests and to promote a patriotic-nationalist agenda. As Putin began his third term, mass political mobilization—when thousands of ordinary Russians called attention to election irregularities, abuses of human rights, and civil and political violations—had become a thing of the past.[44]

For right-wing extremists, the mobilization campaigns of 2012 presented a unique opportunity: to legitimize their marginal status by entering the arena of mass politics in direct opposition to the Kremlin. The odd pairing of right-wing extremists and staunchly pro-democratic activists did not garner much support from either side. Right-wing extremists denounced joint actions with "despised liberals and leftists." In fact, shortly after realizing the futility of influencing state power, most right-wing groups abandoned large-scale protest activity. They went underground, plotting in tight-knit cells the work of a white power revolution. That year, extremist violence continued without interruption, targeting dark-skinned individuals and anyone who did not look "Slavic," particularly at rock and hip-hop concerts, football matches, and other boisterous events that drew large crowds. According to the Sova Center, a leading think tank on racism in post-Soviet Russia, nineteen people died and 187 sustained injuries as a result of right-wing extremist violence.[45]

Raw statistics, however, obscure more than they reveal about the prevalence of racist or exclusionary thinking in ordinary lives. Most ethnic Russians—comprising 80 percent of the population in the Russian Federation according to the 2010 census—did not fully articulate far-right exclusionary and dehumanizing ideologies. They did not indulge in explicit racial fantasies, couched in suggestive or coded language, to protect the homeland from immigration threats or demographic decline. But as Putin embraced a conservative-nationalist agenda, ideas operating on the fringe of society gradually moved to the realm of acceptable discourse.

The elevation of whiteness took place against the backdrop of a conservative turn in Russian politics and society: the normalization of sexism and homophobia in popular consciousness, the strengthening of "traditional family values," and the regulation of family and reproductive behavior. Among other things, biopolitical interventionism provided authorities a set of powerful tools to delineate belonging.[46] The idea of whiteness—and the meanings attached to how white ethnic Russians perceived themselves and those around them resonated powerfully in a variety of different settings: in TV broadcasts and popular jokes, magazine and newspaper advertisements, and the internet; in official and unofficial government practices; and in popular rhetoric, norms, and customs.

Researchers studying ethnic discrimination in post-Soviet Russia have concluded that, while support for white supremacist groups remained low, xenophobic attitudes were unusually widespread, with men more prone to negative, xenophobic feelings than women. In the labor market, especially in Moscow and St. Petersburg, employers consistently preferred to hire applicants with Russified or Europeanized names (as opposed to people whose names were easily recognizable as Caucasian or Central Asian). In the world of popular culture, images of blackness proliferated—with that of Barack Obama one of the most widely circulated. Racist memes and joke culture consistently portrayed Obama as an ape, holding or eating a banana. The crude, filthy visuals of Obama's Black physicality not only colored the forms of the hostility and oppression against him, but also spoke broadly of how the cultural imagination created and reproduced white privilege.[47]

The dominance of whiteness was on wide display in the race-conscious "Slavs Only" (tol'ko slavianam) job advertisements and apartment and room listings as well. One ad for a vacancy at a Moscow café requested that applicants have "at least one year's experience, friendly personality, and a Slavic appearance."[48] The Jewish Museum and Tolerance Center in Moscow made international headlines when it listed "Slavic appearance" as a requirement for a barista opening.[49] Most ethnic disclaimers, however, were reserved for apartment advertisements. A typical listing stipulated that the landowner would

> consider Slavic people only, without pets and small children. It's possible [to rent the apartment] to a friendly, normal group of co-workers from the same firm or who hail from the same city or village. If four or five men [would like to live together], you have nothing to worry about. The most important thing is to look Slavic.[50]

Landlords did not always agree on who was a "Slav" or, for that matter, on who qualified as a citizen of the Russian Federation. Sometimes Belarussians and Ukrainians did not fit the requirement. On other occasions, Moscow landlords confused an individual from, say, Cheliabinsk (the Urals in the Russian Federation) with a labor migrant from Kyrgyzstan. But even with all the uncertainty swirling around definitions, most Russian landlords agreed that people with darker, Caucasian, or Asian features or easily identifiable ethnic names and accents need not apply.

According to an analysis of 32,000 apartment advertisements made by *Novaia gazeta* (New Newspaper), 14 percent of listings in Moscow included the disclaimers "Citizens of the Russian Federation," "Russians Only," and "Slavs Only." In St. Petersburg, the numbers came out lower at around 4 percent, while in Novosibirsk, Samara, Kazan, Nizhnii Novgorod, and Ekaterinburg they totaled at 5 percent. Another study, focusing on Moscow and paying close attention to geography, arrived at a similar conclusion, finding that the highest rates of ethnic discrimination took place in the poorest districts of Moscow, where landlords typically charged the lowest monthly payments for rooms or apartments. Severny, in the northern tip of Moscow, was the capital's most racist neighborhood, with 58 percent of all landlords restricting tenants by Slavic origins. Kapotnia, Vnukovo, and Pechatniki were not too far behind, with approximately 50 percent of all landlords including the ethnic disclaimer in ads.[51]

The apartment listings with "Slavs Only" disclaimers delineated the color line by writing race directly on the body. These markers highlight the challenges and pressures immigrant groups faced in successfully adapting to white mainstream society. Eva Mizrabekyan, who moved to Moscow from Azerbaijan in the late 1990s when her Armenian husband found work at a restaurant, described the difficulties of finding a rental property. "My husband is light-skinned, so sometimes we wouldn't have any problems right away if he went to see the apartment alone," Mizrabekyan said. "But when it was time to sign the agreement the landlord would find out our name and start cursing and would either try to raise the price or back out altogether." Emil Allakhverdiev, an English teacher of Azerbaijani origins, told a journalist that it was not "just the disclaimers that you see in one out of three ads," but also the real estate agents who "hang up the phone" when they hear your last name.[52]

Real estate agencies defended the practice. "It's not discrimination," one real estate agent insisted in an interview with a journalist. "The goal is to prevent migrant workers from Central Asia and southern Russian republics from turning apartments into 'hostels.'"[53] Most ordinary Russians supported the practice as well. "I will tell you why we advertise it here like that," one internet user posted a message in a chat group. "The thing to consider is the reputation of the migrants from the CIS—namely, Kazakhs, Tajiks, Uzbeks, etc. No one wants to rent apartments to them not because they don't respect these nationalities, but because they don't want their apartments torn to

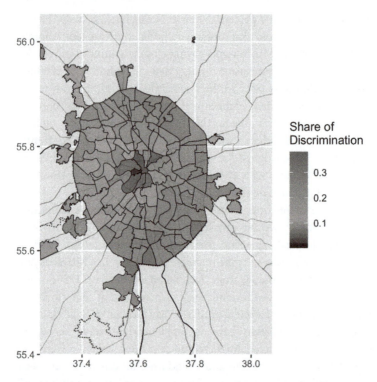

Image 4.3 The percentage of Moscow apartment listings, by neighborhood, which specify the race of potential tenants. According to data compiled by the Robustory project, the most discriminatory neighborhoods were located furthest from the city center, with the lowest property prices. Using the real estate website Cian.ru, Robustory compiled data based on 35,796 listings on April 2, 2017. © Courtesy of Vladimir Avetian.

pieces. Instead of the one or two people named in the lease agreement, they bring an entire crowd [to live in the apartment]."[54]

Putin's administration did not go so far as to implement racial discrimination as official government policy inscribed in law. It did not limit interethnic exchanges or institute practices of segregation in eating places, hotels, theaters, airport waiting rooms, lavatories, schools, and drinking fountains. It did not impose systematic public policies that explicitly segregated the renting or buying of housing.

But it also did not have to go to those extremes. The Russian Constitution guaranteed equal rights and freedoms regardless of sex, race, nationality, property and official status, and place of residence. Article 136 of the Criminal Code outlined a range of hefty fines for violations, while the Labor Code prohibited discrimination in the workplace based on age, sex, ethnicity, religion, or beliefs.[55] Despite these abstract safeguards, the post-Soviet state created an elaborate "web of discrimination" touching many aspects of daily life. In Putin's Russia, racial hierarchies—the distinctions between "black" and "white"—were maintained by social convention rather than by legal practices. Unofficial practices in hiring and housing—the tacit agreement of not offering employment or, more frequently, not renting apartments to people of color—exposed racial fault lines, establishing and preserving inequalities.[56]

The category of Russianness underwent a profound transformation over the years. For decades, the Soviet regime shaped group consciousness around a rich corpus of myths, legends, heroes, and imagery drawn from Soviet Russia's national past. In a society rooted in class and proletarian internationalist values, Bolshevik propaganda conflated "Soviet" with "Russian" sentiments, however paradoxical the pairing may have appeared to outside observers. The efforts were so successful that generations of Russian-speaking schoolchildren, factory workers, bureaucrats, and soldiers in the Soviet Union defined their collective identity—and imagined their place in the federative community—in terms of Russianness. To be sure, Russocentric populist imagery and rhetoric continued to bind people together long after 1991. But at the turn of the twenty-first century, an important shift took place in how ethnic Russians viewed themselves and the world around them: not only in terms of national-historical symbols, myths, and legends, but also through the prism of race and whiteness.[57]

Russianness and whiteness mutually reinforced one another and were often juxtaposed to blackness.[58] "Slavs Only" disclaimers and other race markers played a powerful role in drawing boundaries around populations by a combination of features such as speech, behavior, appearance, and skin color. As Russian society felt increasingly smug in its whiteness, degradation of populations deemed "black" created a sense of community among white, or European, Russians. Populations from the distant peripheries—the Caucasus, Central Asia, and Asian Russia—experienced a sense of difference, if not alienation and harassment, in their daily lives. A society that was largely color-blind had become increasingly conscious of the role that whiteness played in determining social status. By the time Putin began the third term as president, most ethnic Russians had no problems drawing distinct lines between themselves and populations commonly referred to as "blacks."

NOTES

Acknowledgements

1   Gary Shteyngart, "Living in Trump's Soviet Union," *The New Yorker*, November 21, 2016.

Introduction

1   "Biryulyovo Residents Warn of More Unrest," *Moscow Times*, October 15, 2013. https://themoscowtimes.com/news/biryulyovo-residents-warn -of-more-unrest-28599.

2   "Police Capture Azerbaijani Suspected of Moscow Murder," *BBC News*, October 15, 2013. https://www.bbc.com/news/world-europe-2453276 8; and "Pogromy v Biriulëvo v Moskve," *YouTube*, October 14, 2013. https://www.youtube.com/watch?v=r7REsf5xiRA&list=PLYd3FtDW30 zDyoQnNb2cZt6RVqTI_x7Ko&index=5&t=117s.

3   Daniil Kislov, "Fear and Loathing in the Moscow Suburbs," *openDemocracy*, October 17, 2013. https://www.opendemocracy.net/en/ odr/fear-and-loathing-in-moscow-suburbs/.

4   "Violent Anti-Migrant Protests Rock Moscow," *New York Times*, October 13, 2013. https://www.nytimes.com/2013/10/14/world/europe/ violent-anti-migrant-protests-rock-moscow.html.

5   Jens Siegert, "Natives, Foreigners, and Native Foreigners – The Difficult Task of Coexistence in Russia," *Russian Analytical Digest* 141 (December 23, 2013): 8; and Vera Tolz and Sue-Ann Harding, "From 'Compatriots' to 'Aliens': The Changing Coverage of Migration on Russian Television," *The Russian Review* 74, no. 3 (2015): 461, 463.

6   On the term "racialization," see George M. Frederickson, *Racism: A Short History* (Princeton: Princeton University Press, 2002).

Notes

7   For recent works, see Marina Mogilner, *Homo Imperii: A History of Physical Anthropology in Russia* (Lincoln: University of Nebraska Press, 2013); David Rainbow, ed., *Ideologies of Race: Imperial Russia and the Soviet Union in Global Context* (Montreal: McGill-Queen's University Press, 2019); and Jeff Sahadeo, *Voices from the Soviet Edge: Southern Migrants in Leningrad and Moscow* (Ithaca, NY: Cornell University Press, 2019).

8   W. E. B. Du Bois, "Of the Dawn of Freedom," in *Souls of Black Folk: Essays and Sketches* (Chicago: A. C. McClurg & Co, 1903), 13.

9   Nancy Shields Kollmann, *The Russian Empire, 1450-1801* (New York: Oxford University Press, 2017), 451. On mixed marriage and the problem of fixing identity, see, for example, Saule K. Ualiyeva and Adrienne L. Edgar, "In the Laboratory of Peoples' Friendship: Mixed People in Kazakhstan from the Soviet Era to the Present," in *Global Mixed Race*, ed. Rebecca C. King-O'Riain, Stephen Small, Minelle Mahtani, Miri Song, and Paul Spickard (New York: New York University Press, 2014), 68–90.

10 On Soviet ethnography, see Francine Hirsch, "Race Without the Practice of Racial Politics," *Slavic Review* 61, no. 1 (2002): 34. On the relationship between African Americans and the Soviet Union, see Meredith L. Roman, *Opposing Jim Crow: African Americans and the Soviet Indictment of U. S. Racism, 1928-1937* (Lincoln: University of Nebraska Press, 2012); and Kate A. Baldwin, *Beyond the Color Line and the Iron Curtain: Reading Encounters between Black and Red, 1922-1963* (Durham: Duke University Press, 2002). See also Geoffrey Wheeler, *Racial Problems in Soviet Muslim Asia*, 2nd ed. (London: Oxford University Press, 1967).

11 Juliette Cadiot, *Le laboratoire imperial: Russie-URSS, 1870-1940* (Paris: CRNS, 2007).

12 For an exhaustive analysis of Russia's diverse racial landscape, see Mogilner, *Homo Imperii*.

13 Willard Sunderland, "An Empire of Peasants: Empire-Building, Interethnic Interaction, and Ethnic Stereotyping in the Rural World of the Russian Empire, 1800-1850s," in *Imperial Russia: New Histories for the Empire*, ed. Jane Burbank and David Ransel (Bloomington: Indiana University Press, 1998), 181.

14 Vladimir Alexandrov, *Black Russian* (New York: Atlantic Monthly Press, 2013), 59–60.

15 Peter Kolchin, *Unfree Labor: American Slavery and Russian Serfdom* (Cambridge, MA: Harvard University Press, 1987), 180–2, 184–91; and

Amanda Brickell Bellows, *American Slavery and Russian Serfdom in the Post-Emancipation Imagination* (Chapel Hill: The University of North Carolina Press, 2020), 7.

16   Kolchin, *Unfree Labor*, 180.

17   Alison K. Smith, *For the Common Good and Their Own Well-Being: Social Estates in Imperial Russia* (New York: Oxford University Press, 2014); Sheila Fitzpatrick, "Ascribing Class: The Construction of Social Identity in Soviet Russia," *Journal of Modern History* 65, no. 4 (1993): 745–70; and Paul W. Werth, *The Tsar's Foreign Faiths: Toleration and the Fate of Religious Freedom in Imperial Russia* (New York: Oxford University Press, 2014).

18   On the messiness of race, see David R. Roediger, *Working Toward Whiteness: How America's Immigrants Became White* (New York: Basic Books, 2005), 59–72. See also Eric L. Goldstein, *The Price of Whiteness: Jews, Race, and American Identity* (Princeton: Princeton University Press, 2006).

19   See, for example, the suggestive research on commonplace racial slights and other forms of everyday racism by Derald Wing Sue, Christina M. Capodilupo, Gina C. Torino, et al., "Racial Microaggressions in Everyday Life: Implications for Clinical Practice," *American Psychologist* 62, no. 4 (2007): 271–86.

Chapter 1

1   D. N. Anuchin, "O zadachakh i metodakh antropologii," *Russkii antropologicheskii zhurnal* 1 (1902): 72, 82. See also Marina Mogilner, *Homo Imperii: A History of Physical Anthropology in Russia* (Lincoln: University of Nebraska Press, 2013), 101–2.

2   Gerlandine Heng, *The Invention of Race in the European Middle Ages* (Cambridge: Cambridge University Press, 2018); and Francisco Bethencourt, *Racisms: From the Crusades to the Twentieth Century* (Princeton: Princeton University Press, 2013), 159.

3   Ivan Hannaford, *Race: The History of an Idea in the West* (Washington, DC: The Woodrow Wilson Center Press, 1996), 205–33. For a succinct analysis of Blumenbach, see Nell Irvin Painter, *The History of White People* (New York: W. W. Norton & Company, 2010), 72–90.

4   John Efron, *Defenders of the Race: Jewish Doctors and Race Science in Fin-de-Siècle Europe* (New Haven: Yale University Press, 1994); and

Notes

Mitchell B. Hart, *Social Science and the Politics of Modern Jewish Identity* (Stanford: Stanford University Press, 2000).

5   Karl Hall, "Diskursy o rase: Imperskaia Rossiia i zapad v sravnenii," in *Poniatiia o Rossii: K istoricheskoi semantike imperskogo perioda*, ed. Aleksei Miller, Denis Sdvizhkov, and Ingrid Shirle (Moscow: Novoe literaturnoe obozrenie, 2012), 2: 156–61, 191–3.

6   Charles Steinwedel, "To Make a Difference: The Category of Ethnicity in Late Imperial Russian Politics, 1861-1917," in *Russian Modernity: Politics, Knowledge, Practices*, ed. David L. Hoffmann and Yanni Kotsonis (New York: St. Martin's Press, 2000), 67–86; and Werth, *The Tsar's Foreign Faiths*, 171–2.

7   *Nastol'nyi slovar' dlia spravok po vsem otrasliam znaniia* (St. Petersburg: V. Bezobrazov, 1864), 3: 269; and *Russkii entsiklopedicheskii slovar'* (St. Petersburg: Obshchestvennaia pol'za, 1875), 1, pt. 4: 90. The word "race" had not appeared in Russian dictionaries in 1854: *Spravochnyi entsiklopedicheskii slovar'* (St. Petersburg: A. Dmitriev, 1854).

8   Steinwedel, "To Make a Difference," 72.

9   I borrow the phrase "liberal humanism" from H. Glenn Penny and Matti Bunzl, eds., *Worldly Provincialism: German Anthropology in the Age of Empire* (Ann Arbor: University of Michigan Press, 2003), 1. On the liberal turn in Russian ethnography, see Nathaniel Knight, "Science, Empire, and Nationality: Ethnography in the Russian Geographical Society, 1845-1855," in *Imperial Russia: New Histories for the Empire*, ed. Jane Burbank and David L. Ransel (Bloomington: Indiana University Press, 1997), 131.

10 A. M. Sementovskii, *Etnograficheskii obzor Vitebskoi gubernii* (St. Petersburg: M. Khan, 1872), 58.

11 Michael Khodarkovsky, "The Conversion of Non-Christians in Early Modern Russia," in *Of Religion and Empire: Missions, Conversion, and Tolerance in Tsarist Russia*, ed. Robert P. Geraci and Michael Khodarkovsky (Ithaca, NY: Cornell University Press, 2001), 115–43.

12 Werth, *The Tsar's Foreign Faiths*, 82–5.

13 Eugene M. Avrutin, *Jews and the Imperial State: Identification Politics in Tsarist Russia* (Ithaca, NY: Cornell University Press, 2010), 153; ChaeRan Freeze, "When Chava Left Home: Gender, Conversion, and the Jewish Family in Tsarist Russia," *Polin* 18 (2005): 153–88; and Todd M. Endelman, *Leaving the Jewish Fold: Conversion and Radical Assimilation in Modern Jewish History* (Princeton: Princeton University Press, 2015), 326–33.

14   On the rise of statistics in Russia, see Martine Mespoulet, *Statistique et Revolution en Russie: Un Compromise Impossible, 1880-1930* (Rennes: Presses universitaires de Rennes, 2001). For a suggestive study of racial photography, see Amos Morris-Reich, *Race and Photography: Racial Photography as Scientific Evidence, 1876-1980* (Chicago: University of Chicago Press, 2016), as well as Elizabeth Abel, *Signs of the Times: The Visual Politics of Jim Crow* (Berkeley: University of California Press, 2010), 21.

15   D. N. Anuchin, "Beglyi vzgliad na proshloe antropologii i na ee zadachi v Rossii," *Russkii antropologicheskii zhurnal* 1 (1900): 34.

16   Mogilner, *Homo Imperii*, 205.

17   V. L'vovich, ed., *Narody Russkago Tsarstva: Sbornik statei po etnografii. Kniga dlia chteniia doma i v shkole* (Moscow: Pervaia zhenskaia tipografiia E. K. Gerbek, 1901), 584.

18   D. N. Anuchin, *O geograficheskom raspredelenii rosta muzhskogo naseleniia Rossii (po dannym o vseobshchei voinskoi povinnosti v imperii za 1874-1883 gg.): Sravnitel'no s raspredeleniem rosta v drugikh stranakh* (St. Petersburg: V. Bezobrazov, 1889), 113.

19   For Russia, see M. L. Usov, *Predanie i fakty (k evreiskomu voprosu)*, 2nd enl. ed. (St. Petersburg, 1910), 69–79.

20   Quoted in Daniel P. Todes, "Darwin's Malthusian Metaphor and Russian Evolutionary Thought, 1859-1907," *Isis* 78, no. 4 (1987): 546.

21   On Russian national style, Todes, "Darwin's Malthusian Metaphor," 546; and Steven G. Marks, *How Russia Shaped the Modern World: From Art to Anti-Semitism, Ballet to Bolshevism* (Princeton: Princeton University Press, 2003), 140–75.

22   Rana A. Hogarth, *Medicalizing Blackness: Making Racial Difference in the Atlantic World, 1780-1840* (Chapel Hill: The University of North Carolina Press, 2017), 19; and Hart, *Social Science and the Politics of Modern Jewish Identity*, 10–11.

23   "Nervnye i psikhicheskie zabolevaniia," *Evreiskaia entsiklopediia: Svod znanii o evreistve i ego kul'ture v proshlom i nastoiashchem*, 16 vols. (Moscow: Terra, 1991), 11: 669.

24   I. Stavskii, "Shkol'no-patologicheskii tip v evreiskikh uchebnykh zavedeniiakh g. Odessy," *Evreiskii meditsinskii golos* 1–2 (1911): 1–17.

25   For Russia, see Mogilner, *Homo Imperii*. Compare with Alice L. Conklin, *In the Museum of Man: Race, Anthropology, and Empire in France, 1850-1950* (Ithaca, NY: Cornell University Press, 2013).

26   See, for example, Anatolii P. Bogdanov's translations of Broca's work printed in two installments: Paul Broca, comp., *Antropologicheskie*

Notes

tablitsy dlia kraniologicheskikh i kefalometricheskikh vychislenii, trans. and ed. Anatolii P. Bogdanov (Moscow: S. P. Arkhipov, 1879). On Broca, see Conklin, *In the Museum of Man*, 96–100. On Bogdanov, see D. N. Anuchin, "Nekrolog A. P. Bogdanov," in *D. N. Anuchin o liudiakh russkoi nauki i kul'tury: Stat'i, nekrologi, i zametki*, ed. A. V. Artsikhovskii (Moscow: Gosudarstvennoe izdatel'stvo geograficheskoi literatury, 1950), 237–55.

27   L. D. Alekseeva, "Moskovskii universitet i stanovlenie prepodavaniia etnografii v dorevoliutsionnoi Rossii," *Vestnik Moskovskogo universiteta*, series 8, no. 6 (1983): 54–62; V. V. Bogdanov, *D. N. Anuchin, antropolog i geograf (1843-1923)* (Moscow: Moskovskoe obshchestvo ispytatelei prirody, 1940); and G. V. Karpov, *Dmitrii Nikolaevich Anuchin* (Moscow: Izdatel'stvo Moskovskogo universiteta, 1962), 8–11.

28   Anuchin, "Beglyi vzgliad na proshloe antropologii i na ee zadachi v Rossii," 38. On German anthropology's provincial worldliness, see Penny and Bunzl, eds., *Worldly Provincialism*.

29   A. A. Ivanovskii, "Ob antropologicheskom izuchenii inorodcheskogo naseleniia Rossii," *Russkii antropologicheskii zhurnal* 1 (1902): 112.

30   Anuchin, "Beglyi vzgliad na proshloe antropologii i na ee zadachi v Rossii," 30.

31   Ivanovskii, "Ob antropologicheskom izuchenii inorodcheskogo naseleniia Rossii," 116.

32   A. A. Ivanovskii, "Opyt antropologicheskoi klassifikatsii naseleniia Rossii," *Russkii antropologicheskii zhurnal* 3/4 (1903): 107–8.

33   Ivanovskii, "Opyt antropologicheskoi klassifikatsii naseleniia Rossii," 152, 158.

34   A. D. El'kind, *Antropologicheskoe izuchenie evreev za poslednie desiat' let* (Moscow: P. P. Riabushinskii, 1912), 1. See also El'kind's "Evrei," *Russkii antropologicheskii zhurnal* 3 (1902): 41–2.

35   R. L. Veinberg, "K izucheniiu o forme mozga cheloveka," *Russkii antropologicheskii zhurnal* 4 (1902): 1–4, 12, 20–1.

36   Mikhail Georgievich Iakovenko, *Materialy k antropologii evreiskogo naseleniia Rogacheskogo uezda, Mogilevskoi gubernii* (St. Petersburg: Tipografiia Ministerstva putei soobshcheniia, 1898), 48–50.

37   Frank Dikötter, "Race Culture: Recent Perspectives on the History of Eugenics," *American Historical Review* 103, no. 2 (1998): 467–78.

38   On the transmission of ideas, see Ulinka Rublack, *Reformation Europe* (Cambridge: Cambridge University Press, 2005), 46.

Chapter 2

1 L. E. Gorizontov, *Paradoksy imperskoi politiki: Poliaki v Rossii i russkie v Pol'she* (Moscow: Izdatel'stvo "Indrik," 1999), 100–8; and Dominic Lieven, *Empire: The Russian Empire and Its Rivals* (New Haven: Yale University Press, 2000), 200–1. On Russification practices, see Edward C. Thaden, "Administrative Russification in the Baltic Provinces, 1855-1881," in *Russification in the Baltic Provinces and Finland, 1855-1914*, ed. Thaden (Princeton: Princeton University Press, 1881), 33–53.

2 Richard S. Wortman, *Scenarios of Power: Myth and Ceremony in Russian Monarchy*, vol. 2 (Princeton: Princeton University Press, 2000), 236–8, 262. For a broader pan-European perspective, see Neil MacMaster, *Racism in Europe, 1870-2000* (Basingtoke: Palgrave Macmillan, 2001), 20–1.

3 Quoted in John D. Klier, *Russians, Jews, and the Pogroms of 1881-1882* (Cambridge: Cambridge University Press, 2011), 139, 141.

4 On the role of Jews in the revolutionary movement, see Erich Haberer, *Jews and Revolution in Nineteenth-Century Russia* (Cambridge: Cambridge University Press, 1995).

5 Yuri Slezkine, *The Jewish Century* (Princeton: Princeton University Press, 2004), 114–26.

6 Klier, *Russians, Jews, and the Pogroms of 1881-1882*, 182.

7 Robert Geraci, "Pragmatism and Prejudice: Revisiting the Origin of the Pale of Jewish Settlement and Its Historiography," *The Journal of Modern History* 91, no. 4 (2019): 776–814.

8 *Nedel'naia khronika voskhoda* 41 (1887): 1025.

9 Henrik B. Sliozberg, *Pravovoe i ekonomicheskoe polozhenie Evreev v Rossii* (St. Petersburg: Levenstein, 1907), 97–100; and Eugene M. Avrutin, *Jews and the Imperial State: Identification Politics in Tsarist Russia* (Ithaca, NY: Cornell University Press, 2010), 169–79.

10 Quoted in Benjamin Nathans, *Beyond the Pale: The Jewish Encounter with Late Imperial Russia* (Berkeley: University of California Press, 2002), 258–9.

11 Natan M. Meir, *Kiev, Jewish Metropolis: A History, 1859-1914* (Bloomington: Indiana University Press, 2010), 196–7. Nathans offers the most detailed analysis of the quota system in higher education in *Beyond the Pale*, 257–307. See also Willard Sunderland, *The Baron's Cloak: A History of the Russian Empire in War and Revolution* (Ithaca, NY: Cornell University Press, 2014), 47–8.

Notes

12 Vladimir Alexandrov, *The Black Russian* (New York: Atlantic Monthly Press, 2013).

13 Darius Staliūnas, *Making Russians: Meaning and Practice of Russification in Lithuania and Belarus after 1863* (Amsterdam: Rodopi, 2007), 90–5; Mikhail Dolbilov, *Russkii krai, chuzhaia vera: Etnokonfessional'naia politika v Litve i Belorussii pri Alexandre II* (Moscow: Novoe literanurnoe obozrenie, 2010), 391; and Andrew A. Gentes, *The Mass Deportation of Poles to Siberia, 1863-1880* (Basingtoke: Palgrave Macmillan, 2017), 78, 83–4.

14 Hans Rogger, *Jewish Policies and Right-Wing Politics in Imperial Russia* (Berkeley: University of California Press, 1986), 35–6; Meir, *Kiev, Jewish Metropolis*, 199–208; Jeffrey Veidlinger, *Jewish Public Culture in the Late Russian Empire* (Bloomington: Indiana University Press, 2009), 63–4; and Faith Hillis, *Children of Rus': Right-Bank Ukraine and the Invention of a Russian Nation* (Ithaca, NY: Cornell University Press, 2013), 141, 144.

15 Eugene M. Avrutin, "Returning to Judaism after the 1905 Law on Religious Freedom in Tsarist Russia," *Slavic Review* 65, no. 1 (2006): 90–110.

16 For similarities with Germany and Austria-Hungary, see Todd M. Endelman, *Leaving the Jewish Fold: Conversion and Radical Assimilation in Modern Jewish History* (Princeton: Princeton University Press), 88–146.

17 Avrutin, *Jews and the Imperial State*, 121.

18 "Petition of Sofiia Zil'berman of Dvinsk to Change Jewish Surnames of Converted Children," in *Everyday Jewish Life in Imperial Russia: Select Documents*, ed. ChaeRan Y. Freeze and Jay M. Harris (Waltham: Brandeis University Press, 2013), 240–1.

19 Quoted in Jacob Langer, "Corruption and the Counterrevolution: The Rise and Fall of the Black Hundred," PhD Dissertation, Duke University, 2007, 47.

20 Hillis, *Children of Rus'*, 170–1.

21 George Gilbert, *The Radical Right in Late Imperial Russia: Dreams of a True Fatherland?* (London: Routledge, 2016), 52–86; and Langer, "Corruption and the Counterrevolution," 63.

22 Gilbert, *The Radical Right in Late Imperial Russia*, 119–21; and Hillis, *Children of Rus'*, 216–18.

23 Leopold H. Haimson and Ronald Petrusha, "Two Strike Waves in Imperial Russia, 1905-1907, 1912-1914," in *Strikes, Wars, and Revolutions in an International Perspective: Strike Waves in the Late*

Nineteenth and Early Twentieth Centuries, ed. Leopold H. Haimson and Charles Tilly (Cambridge: Cambridge University Press, 1989), 145.

24 Jonathan Daly, "Government, Press, and Subversion in Russia, 1906-1917," *The Journal of the Historical Society* 9, no. 1 (2009): 38-9.

25 Mark D. Steinberg, *Petersburg Fin de* Siècle (New Haven: Yale University Press, 2011), 235.

26 Joan Neuberger, *Hooliganism: Crime, Culture, and Power in St. Petersburg, 1900-1914* (Berkeley: University of California Press, 1993), 71-110.

27 Shlomo Lambroza, "The Pogroms of 1903-1906" and Robert Weinberg, "The Pogrom of 1905 in Odessa: A Case Study," in *Pogroms: Anti-Jewish Violence in Modern Russian History*, ed. John D. Klier and Shlomo Lambroza (Cambridge: Cambridge University Press, 1992), 226-31, 248-89.

28 Robert Weinberg, "The Russian Right Responds to 1905: Visual Depictions of Jews in Postrevolutionary Russia," in *The Revolution of 1905 and Russia's Jews*, ed. Stefani Hoffman and Ezra Mendelsohn (Philadelphia: University of Pennsylvania Press, 2008), 53-69. For a suggestive analysis of the social and cultural reverberations of anti-Semitism, see Hillel J. Kieval, "Afterward: European Antisemitism—The Search for a Pattern," in *Sites of European Antisemitism in the Age of Mass Politics, 1880-1918*, ed. Robert Nemes and Daniel Unowsky (Waltham, MA: Brandeis University Press, 2014), 260.

29 This chapter does not discuss the Muslim Question. Around fifteen million Muslims resided in the empire, mostly along the southern border, in Central Asia, the North Caucasus, and the Kazakh Steppe. For two contrasting views, specifically in comparison to Jews, see Robert Crews, "Fear and Loathing in the Russian Empire," in *Antisemitism and Islamophobia in Europe: A Shared Story?* ed. James Renton and Ben Gidley (Basingtoke: Palgrave Macmillan, 2017), 79-98; and Yohanan Petrovsky Shtern, "Jewish Apples and Muslim Oranges in the Russian Basket," in *Jews and Muslims in the Russian Empire and the Soviet Union*, ed. Franziska Davies, Martin Schulze Wessel, and Michael Brenner (Gottingen: Vandenhoeck & Ruprecht, 2015), 23.

30 On the commonalities between the Yellow Peril and anti-Jewish prejudice, see Sunderland, *The Baron's Cloak*, 98-9; and Vadim Rossman, "Prizraki IX veka: 'Zheltaia opasnost' i evreiskii zagovor v evropeiskikh stsenariiakh zakaty Evropy," *Paralleli* 2-3 (2003): 11-52.

31 Quoted in David Schimmelpenninck van der Oye, *Toward the Rising Sun: Russian Ideologies of Empire and the Path to War with Japan*

(DeKalb: Northern Illinois University Press, 2006), 206. See also Sergey Glebov, "Between Foreigners and Subjects: Imperial Subjecthood, Governance, and the Chinese in the Russian Far East," *Ab Imperio* 1 (2017): 114–15.

32   Anatolii Remnev, "Colonization and 'Russification' in the Imperial Geography of Asiatic Russia: From the Nineteenth to the Early Twentieth Centuries," in *Asiatic Russia: Imperial Power in Regional and International Contexts*, ed. Tomohiko Uyama (London: Routledge, 2012), 105–6; and Paul W. Werth, "Human Mobility in Russia's Asian Empire," in *Empire in Asia: A New Global History*, ed. Donna Brunero and Brian P. Farrell (London: Bloomsbury, 2018), 187–214.

33   Lewis H. Siegelbaum, "Another 'Yellow Peril': Chinese Migrants in the Russian Far East and the Russian Reaction before 1917," *Modern Asian Studies* 12, no. 2 (1978): 307–30; and Alyssa M. Park, *Sovereignty Experiments: Korean Migrants and the Building of Borders in Northeast Asia*, 1860-1945 (Ithaca, NY: Cornell University Press, 2019), 126–8, 167–8.

34   Glebov, "Between Foreigners and Subjects," 113. Similarly, California immigration restrictions played an important role in the passage of the Immigration Restriction Act in Victoria. See, for example, Marilyn Lake and Henry Reynolds, *Drawing the Global Colour Line: White Men's Countries and the International Challenge of Racial Equality* (Cambridge: Cambridge University Press, 2008), 15–45. For a recent analysis of Chinese exclusion in the United States, see Beth Lew-Williams, *The Chinese Must Go: Violence, Exclusion, and the Making of the Alien in America* (Cambridge, MA: Harvard University Press, 2018).

35   For a global analysis of border control, see Adam M. McKeown, *Melancholy Order: Asian Migration and the Globalization of Borders* (New York: Columbia University Press, 2008), 121–46.

36   David Wolff, "Russia Finds its Limits: Crossing Borders into Manchuria," in *Rediscovering Russia in Asia: Siberia and the Russian Far East*, ed. Stephen Kotkin and David Wolff (Armonk: M. E. Sharpe, 1995), 42; and John J. Stephan, *The Russian Far East: A History* (Stanford: Stanford University Press, 1994), 72–3.

37   Quoted in Iana Sergeevna Gusei, "'Zheltaia Opasnost': Predstavleniia ob ugroze s vostoka v Rossiiskoi Imperii v kontse XIX—nachale XX v.," PhD Dissertation, European University in St. Petersburg, 2014, 71. See also Anna Bek, *The Life of a Russian Woman Doctor: A Siberian Memoir, 1869*-1954, transl. and ed. by Anne D. Rassweiler (Bloomington: Indiana University Press, 2004), 87.

38   Sören Urbansky, *Beyond the Steppe Frontier: A History of the Sino-Russian Border* (Princeton: Princeton University Press, 2020), 39–63.

39   Park, *Sovereignty Experiments*, 131.

40   Michael Keevak, *Becoming Yellow: A Short History of Racial Thinking* (Princeton: Princeton University Press, 2011), 125–6.

41   Schimmelpenninck van der Oye, *Toward the Rising Sun*, 34–5.

42   Chia Yin Hsu, "A Tale of Two Railroads: 'Yellow Labor', Agrarian Colonization, and the Making of Russianness at the Far Eastern Frontier, 1890s-1910s," *Ab Imperio* 3 (2006): 225–6. On Leland Stanford, see Gordon H. Chang, *Ghosts of Gold Mountain: The Epic Story of the Chinese Who Built the Transcontinental Railroad* (New York: Houghton Mifflin Harcourt, 2019), 61–2.

43   Siegelbaum, "Another 'Yellow Peril,'" 322; and Abraham Ascher, *P. A. Stolypin: The Search for Stability in Late Imperial Russia* (Stanford: Stanford University Press, 2001), 326.

44   Cemil Aydin, *The Politics of Anti-Westernism in Asia: Visions of World Order in Pan-Islamic and Pan-Asian Thought* (New York: Columbia University Press, 2007), 71–8; and W. E. B. Du Bois, "The Color Line Belts the World," in *W. E. B. Du Bois on Asia: Crossing the World Color Line*, ed. Bill V. Mullen and Cathryn Watson (Jackson, MS: University Press of Mississippi, 2005), 34.

45   Gusei, "Zheltaia Opasnost," 156.

46   Stephen M. Norris, *A War of Images: Russian Popular Prints, Wartime Culture, and National Identity, 1812-1945* (DeKalb: Northern Illinois University Press, 2006), 107–15; and Susanna Soojung Lim, *China and Japan in the Russian Imagination, 1685-1922* (London: Routledge, 2013), 142–6.

47   RGIA, f. 1276, op. 9, d. 28, ll. 2-3, 5, 8; and V. Mikhailov, *Tret'ia gosudarstvennaia duma i zheltaia opasnost'* (St. Petersburg: Tipografiia R. V. Korotaevoi, 1912), 10–11.

48   Evelyn Hu-Dehart, "Chinese Labor Migrants to the Americas in the Nineteenth Century: An Inquiry into Who They Were and the World They Left Behind," in *The Chinese and the Iron Road: Building the Transcontinental Railroad*, ed. Gordon H. Chang and Shelley Fisher Fishkin (Stanford: Stanford University Press, 2019), 42–52. See also Naja Aarim-Heriot, *Chinese Immigrants, African Americans, and Racial Anxiety in the United States, 1848-1882* (Urbana: University of Illinois, 2003).

49   Siegelbaum, "Another 'Yellow Peril,'" 325; and Park, *Sovereignty Experiments*, 138.

Notes

50 RGIA, f. 1276, op. 7, d. 11, 1-1ob, 7; and RGIA, f. 37, op. 44, d. 2631, ll. 18-18ob, 24ob. See also Urbansky, *Beyond the Steppe Frontier*, 83–5; and Park, *Sovereignty Experiments*, 141.

51 Remnev, "Colonization and 'Russification' in the Imperial Geography of Asiatic Russia," 113.

52 RGIA, f. 391, op. 10, d. 297, ll. 2ob-3, 27.

53 Harriet Murav, "The Predatory Jew and Russian Vitalism: Dostoevsky, Rozanov, and Babel," in *Ritual Murder in Russia, Eastern Europe, and Beyond: New Histories of an Old Accusation*, ed. Eugene M. Avrutin, Jonathan Dekel-Chen, and Robert Weinberg (Bloomington: Indiana University Press, 2017): 151–71; and Vera Tolz, "Discourses of Race in Imperial Russia (1830-1914)," in *The Invention of Race: Scientific and Popular Representations*, ed. Nicolas Bancel, Thomas David, and Dominic Thomas (New York: Routledge, 2014), 130–44.

54 Mark B. Adams, "Eugenics in Russia, 1900-1940," in *The Wellborn Science: Eugenics in Germany, France, Brazil, and Russia*, ed. Adams (Oxford: Oxford University Press, 1990), 6.

55 *Kratkoe rukovodstvo dlia antropologicheskikh izmerenii s tsel'iu opredeleniia retsidistov, sostavlennoe po sisteme Bertil'ona (izdano po rasporiazheniiu S. Peterburgskogo gradonachal'nika)* (St. Petersburg: Tipografiia Kantseliarii S. Peterburgskogo gradonachal'nika, 1891).

56 Robert Weinberg, *Blood Libel in Late Imperial Russia: The Ritual Murder Trial of Mendel Beilis* (Bloomington: Indiana University Press, 2014), 87; and Hillis, *Children of Rus'*, 246.

57 Hillel J. Kieval, "The Rules of the Game: Forensic Medicine and the Language of Science in the Structuring of Modern Ritual Murder Trials," *Jewish History* 26, no. 3–4 (2012): 287–307.

58 Marina Mogilner, *Homo Imperii: A History of Physical Anthropology in Russia* (Lincoln: University of Nebraska Press, 2013), 170–5, 179.

59 Weinberg, *Blood Libel in Late Imperial Russia*, 152.

60 Weinberg, *Blood Libel in Late Imperial Russia*, 164–5.

61 Semen Gol'din, *Russkaia armiia i evrei, 1914-1917* (Moscow: Mosty kul'tury, 2018), 111–12.

62 On forced deportations and accusations of spying, see Eric Lohr, *Nationalizing the Russian Empire: The Campaign against Enemy Aliens during World War I* (Cambridge, MA: Harvard University Press, 2003), 17–21. On anti-Chinese measures, see RGIA, f. 1276, op. 11, d. 1453, l. 3.

Chapter 3

1   Claude McKay, *A Long Way from Home* (New York: Arno Press, 1969), 150; and Kate A. Baldwin, *Beyond the Color Line and the Iron Curtain: Reading Encounters between Black and Red, 1922-1963* (Durham: Duke University Press, 2002), 37. For a recent analysis of the Comintern, see Steven S. Lee, "Introduction: Comintern Aesthetics—Space, Form, History," in *Comintern Aesthetics*, ed. Amelia M. Glaser and Steven S. Lee (Toronto: University of Toronto Press, 2020), 3–5.

2   McKay, *A Long Way from Home*, 170, 173; and Wayne F. Cooper, *Claude McKay: Rebel Sojourner in the Harlem Renaissance* (Baton Rouge: Louisiana State University Press, 1987), 174–89.

3   McKay, *A Long Way from Home*, 167–8.

4   Claude McKay, "Soviet Russia and the Negro," *The Crisis* 27, no. 3 (1924): 114–15.

5   Robert V. Daniels, ed., *A Documentary History of Communism in Russia: From Lenin to Gorbachev* (Hanover: University Press of New England, 1993), 66–7.

6   Allison Blakely, *Russia and the Negro: Blacks in Russian History and Thought* (Washington, DC: Howard University Press, 1986), 81. See also Meredith L. Roman, *Opposing Jim Crow: African Americans and the Soviet Indictment of U.S. Racism, 1928-1937* (Lincoln: University of Nebraska Press, 2012). On the global color line, see Marilyn Lake and Henry Reynolds, *Drawing the Global Colour Line: White Men's Countries and the International Challenge of Racial Equality* (Cambridge: Cambridge University Press, 2008).

7   For a short overview, see William G. Rosenberg, "Problems of Social Welfare and Everyday Life," in *Critical Companion to the Russian Revolution, 1914-1921*, ed. Howard Acton, Vladimir Iu. Cherniaev, and William G. Rosenberg (Bloomington: Indiana University Press, 1997), 633–44.

8   For a recent overview of the civil war pogroms, see Laura Engelstein, *Russia in Flames: War, Revolution, Civil War, 1914-1921* (New York: Oxford University Press, 2018), 511–40.

9   Elissa Bemporad and Thomas Chopard, "Introduction: The Pogroms of the Russian Civil War at 100," *Quest: Issues in Contemporary Jewish History* 15 (2019): xiv; and Oleg Budnitskii, *Russian Jews Between the Reds and the Whites, 1917-1920*, trans. Timothy J. Price (Philadelphia: University of Pennsylvania Press, 2012), 217–9.

Notes

10   For an overview of paramilitary violence in comparative perspective, see Robert Gerwarth and John Horne, "Vectors of Violence: Paramilitarism in Europe after the Great War, 1917-1923," *Journal of Modern History* 83, no. 3 (2011): 489–512.

11   Lidia B. Miliakova, ed., *Kniga pogromov: Pogromy na Ukraine, v Belorussii i evropeiskoi chasti Rossii v period Grazhdanskoi voiny, 1918-1922 gg. Sbornik dokumentov.* (Moscow: ROSSPEN, 2007), 51, 551–2, 562, 633.

12   Thomas Chopard, "Ukrainian Neighbors: Pogroms and Extermination in Ukraine, 1919-1920," *Quest: Issues in Contemporary Jewish History* 15 (2019): 139–67.

13   Quoted in Brendan McGeever, *Antisemitism and the Russian Revolution* (Cambridge: Cambridge University Press, 2019), 78–9.

14   Vladimir Il'ich Lenin, "Speeches on Gramophone Records: Anti-Jewish Pogroms," in *Lenin and the Jewish Question*, ed. Hyman Lumer (New York: International Publishers, 1974), 135.

15   Elissa Bemporad, *Legacy of Blood: Jews, Pogroms, and Ritual Murder in the Lands of the Soviets* (New York: Oxford University Press, 2019), 27–31, 62–6; and Gennady Estraikh, "Simulating Justice: The Blood Libel Case in Moscow, April 1922," in *Ritual Murder in Russia, Eastern Europe, and Beyond: New Histories of an Old Accusation*, ed. Eugene M. Avrutin, Jonathan Dekel-Chen, and Robert Weinberg (Bloomington: Indiana University Press, 2017), 204–18.

16   I. M. Rubinow, "Lessons from Russia," *The Crisis* 4 (1912): 194.

17   Daniel B. Schwartz, *Ghetto: The History of a Word* (Cambridge, MA: Harvard University Press, 2019), 166–9.

18   Quoted in Arnold Shankman, "Brothers Across the Sea: Afro-Americans on the Persecution of Russian Jews, 1881-1917," *Jewish Social Studies* 37, no. 2 (1975): 114–15.

19   W. E. B. Du Bois, *Russia and America: An Interpretation, 1950*, 21, 155, Unpublished Manuscript, W. E. B. Du Bois Papers (MS 312), Special Collections and University Archives, University of Massachusetts Amherst Libraries.

20   W. E. B. Du Bois, "Judging Russia," *The Crisis* 33, no. 4 (1927): 189.

21   Du Bois, *Russia and America*, 27. See also David Levering Lewis, *W. E. B. Du Bois: The Fight for Equality and the American Century, 1919-1963* (New York: Henry Holt and Company, 2000), 197–204.

22   William L. Patterson, *The Man Who Cried Genocide: An Autobiography* (New York: International Publishers, 1971), 112. On KUTV, see Rossen

Djagalov, *From Internationalism to Postcolonialism: Literature and Cinema between the Second and the Third Worlds* (Montreal: McGill-Queen's University Press, 2020), 43–52.

23   Quoted in Eric S. McDuffie, *Sojourning for Black Freedom: Black Women, American Communism, and the Making of Black Left Feminism* (Durham, NC: Duke University Press, 2011), 67.

24   Quoted in Glenda Elizabeth Gilmore, *Defying Dixie: The Radical Roots of Civil Rights, 1919-1950* (New York: W. W. Norton & Company, 2009), 147.

25   Baldwin, *Beyond the Color Line and the Iron Curtain*, 14.

26   For the wider context of diplomacy and internationalism, see Michael David-Fox, *Showcasing the Great Experiment: Cultural Diplomacy and Western Visitors to the Soviet Union, 1921-1941* (New York: Oxford University Press, 2012); and Steven S. Lee, *The Ethnic Avant-Garde: Minority Cultures and World Revolution* (New York: Columbia University Press, 2015).

27   Harry Haywood, *Black Bolshevik: Autobiography of an Afro-Communist* (Chicago: Liberator Press, 1978), 83, 137, 174–5, 339.

28   Langston Hughes, *I Wonder as I Wander: An Autobiographical Journey* (New York: Hill and Wang, 1993), 73, 75, 87.

29   Christina Kiaer, "African Americans in Soviet Socialist Realism: The Case of Aleksandr Deineka," *The Russian Review* 75, no. 3 (2016): 406, 410–1.

30   Roman, *Opposing Jim Crow*, 99–102; and Christina Kiaer, "A Comintern Aesthetics of Anti-racism in the Animated Short Film *Blek end uait*," *Comintern Aesthetics*, 352–83. See also Kiaer's "Anti-racism in Early Soviet Visual Culture," forum on Black Perspectives (online journal of the African American Intellectual History Society), October 31, 2017. https://www.aaihs.org/anti-racism-in-early-soviet-visual-culture/.

31   On the Scottsboro case, see Gilmore, *Defying Dixie*, 126; and Roman, *Opposing Jim Crow*, 99–102.

32   Woodford McClellan, "Africans and Black Americans in the Comintern Schools, 1925-1934," *The International Journal of African Historical Studies* 26, no. 2 (1993): 382, 385.

33   Haywood, *Black Bolshevik*, 169.

34   Blakely, *Russia and the Negro*, 97.

35   Francine Hirsch, *Empire of Nations: Ethnographic Knowledge and the Making of the Soviet Union* (Ithaca, NY: Cornell University Press, 2005), 43, 66; and S. A. Smith, *Russia in Revolution: An Empire in Crisis, 1890-1928* (Oxford: Oxford University Press 2017), 162.

Notes

36 Terry Martin, *The Affirmative Action Empire: Nations and Nationalism in the Soviet Union, 1923-1939* (Ithaca, NY: Cornell University Press, 2001), 17, 32.

37 Hirsch, *Empire of Nations*, 106–44.

38 Martin, *The Affirmative Action Empire*, 449–51.

39 On urban migration, see Lewis H. Siegelbaum and Leslie Page Moch, *Broad Is My Native Land: Repertoires and Regimes of Migration in Russia's Twentieth Century* (Ithaca, NY: Cornell University Press, 2014), 111–21.

40 Gijs Kessler, "The Passport System and State Control over Population Flows in the Soviet Union, 1932-1940," *Cahiers du Monde Russe* 43, no. 2–4 (2001): 477–504.

41 David Shearer, "Elements Near and Alien: Passportization, Policing, and Identity in the Stalinist State," *Journal of Modern History* 76, no. 4 (2004): 838, 846–7.

42 Peter Holquist, "State Violence as Technique: The Logic of Violence in Soviet Totalitarianism," in *Landscaping the Human Garden: Twentieth-Century Population Management in a Comparative Framework*, ed. Amir Weiner (Stanford: Stanford University Press, 2003), 38–44. See also Hirsch, *Empire of Nations*, 231–308.

43 Andrew Sloin, *The Jewish Revolution in Belorussia: Economy, Race, and Bolshevik Power* (Bloomington: Indiana University Press, 2017), 16.

44 Many modern states deployed race to generate or reproduce difference on the basis of ethnic origins. The ideas and practices worked out under the Nazis found broad parallels in overseas colonial settings, in Europe's borderland policies, and the United States. Devin O. Pendas, "Racial States in Comparative Perspective," in *Beyond the Racial State: Rethinking Nazi Germany*, ed. Devin O. Pendas, Mark Roseman, and Richard F. Wetzell (Cambridge: Cambridge University Press, 2017), 116–43. For a novel perspective on the language and practice of racial politics in Soviet life, see Eric D. Weitz, "Racial Politics without the Concept of Race: Reevaluating Ethnic and National Purges," *Slavic Review* 61, no. 1 (2002): 1–29.

45 Martin, *The Affirmative Action Empire*, 340. Martin most likely oversimplifies when making the argument that Soviet xenophobia was driven solely by ideology and suspicions of foreign capitalist government.

46 For the broader argument, see Amir Weiner, *Making Sense of War: The Second World War and the Fate of the Bolshevik Revolution* (Princeton: Princeton University Press, 2001), 147–9.

47 Jörg Baberowski and Anselm Doering-Manteuffel, "The Quest for Order and the Pursuit of Terror: Nationalist Socialist Germany and the Stalinist Soviet Union as Multiethnic Empires," in *Beyond Totalitarianism: Stalinism and Nazism Compared*, ed. Michael Geyer and Sheila Fitzpatrick (Cambridge: Cambridge University Press, 2009), 218–19.

48 Sören Urbansky, *Beyond the Steppe Frontier: A History of the Sino-Russian Border* (Princeton: Princeton University Press, 2020), 164–76.

49 Alyssa M. Park, *Sovereignty Experiments: Korean Migrants and the Building of Borders in Northeast Asia, 1860-1945* (Ithaca, NY: Cornell University Press, 2019), 238–45. See also Michael Gelb, "An Early Soviet Ethnic Deportation: The Far-Eastern Koreans," *Russian Review* 54, no. 3 (1995): 389–412.

50 Jeronim Perovic, *From Conquest to Deportation: The North Caucasus under Russian Rule* (New York: Oxford University Press, 2018), 285.

51 Holquist, "State Violence as Technique," 32–8; Shearer, "Elements Near and Alien," 845–6; and Sheila Fitzpatrick, *Tear Off the Masks! Identity and Imposture in Twentieth-Century Russia* (Princeton: Princeton University Press, 2005), 271.

52 For a suggestive analysis of passports and racial grooming in Nazi Germany, see Peter Fritzsche, *Life and Death in the Third Reich* (Cambridge, MA: Harvard University Press, 2008), 76–82.

53 Robert Weinberg, *Stalin's Forgotten Zion: Birobidzhan and the Making of a Soviet Jewish Homeland* (Berkeley: University of California Press, 1998).

54 Elissa Bemporad, *Becoming Soviet Jews: The Bolshevik Experiment in Minsk* (Bloomington: Indiana University Press, 2013).

55 Mordechai Altshuler, *Soviet Jewry on the Eve of the Holocaust: A Social and Demographic Profile* (Jerusalem: The Centre of East European Jewry, 1998), 12–15, 115. For a wider discussion, see Yuri Slezkine, *The Jewish Century* (Princeton: Princeton University Press, 2004), 216–27.

56 Stephen Kotkin, *Stalin: Paradoxes of Power, 1878-1928* (New York: Penguin Books, 2014), 736.

57 Sloin, *The Jewish Revolution in Belorussia*, 221–37.

58 Kate Brown, *A Biography of No Place: From Ethnic Borderland to Soviet Heartland* (Cambridge, MA: Harvard University Press, 2004), 209.

59 Brown, *A Biography of No Place*, 209–10.

Notes

60   Joshua Rubenstein and Ilya Altman, ed., *The Unknown Black Book: The Holocaust in the German-Occupied Soviet Territories* (Bloomington: Indiana University Press, 2008), 361, 394.

61   Tony Judt, *Postwar: A History of Europe since 1945* (New York: Penguin, 2005), 18–21; Philip Hanson, *The Rise and Fall of the Soviet Economy* (New York: Routledge, 2003), 21–5; and Elena Zubkova, *Russia After the War: Hopes, Illusions and Disappointments*, trans. Hugh Ragsdale (New York: Routledge, 1998), 21–4.

62   Franziska Exeler, "What Did You Do during the War? Personal Responses to the Aftermath of Nazi Occupation," *Kritika: Explorations in Russian and Eurasian History* 17, no. 4 (2016): 815, 826–32; and Elana Jakel, "Ukraine without Jews? Nationality and Belonging in Soviet Ukraine, 1943-1948," PhD diss., University of Illinois, Urbana-Champaign, 2014, 39–54. See also Martin Dean, *Robbing the Jews: The Confiscation of Jewish Property in the Holocaust, 1933-1945* (New York: Cambridge University Press, 2008), 191–6.

63   Emil Draitser, *Shush! A Memoir Growing Up Jewish Under Stalin* (Berkeley: University of California Press, 2008), 11–13.

64   Mary M. Leder, *My Life in Stalinist Russia: An American Woman Looks Back*, ed. Laurie Bernstein (Bloomington: Indiana University Press, 2001), 301.

65   Weiner, *Making Sense of War*, 195.

66   Quoted in Joshua Rubenstein, *The Last Days of Stalin* (New Haven: Yale University Press, 2016), 62.

67   Quoted in Slezkine, *The Jewish Century*, 309–10.

68   Quoted in Anna Shternshis, *When Sonia Met Boris: An Oral History of Jewish Life under Stalin* (New York: Oxford University Press, 2017), 118, 119–20.

69   Quoted in Zvi Gitelman, *Jewish Identities in Postcommunist Russia and Ukraine: An Uncertain Ethnicity* (Cambridge: Cambridge University Press, 2012), 278–9. On friendship of the peoples, see Martin, *Affirmative Action Empire*, 432–61.

70   Adrienne Edgar, "Children of Mixed Marriage in Soviet Central Asia: Dilemmas of Identity and Belonging," in *Ideologies of Race: Imperial Russia and the Soviet Union in Global Context*, ed. David Rainbow (Montreal: McGill-Queen's University Press, 2019), 208. On miscegenation law in America, see Peggy Pascoe, *What Comes Naturally: Miscegenation Law and the Making of Race in America* (New York: Oxford University Press, 2009).

71   Mark Tolts, "Demography of the Jews in the Former Soviet Union: Yesterday and Today," in *Jewish Life after the USSR*, ed. Zvi Gitelman (Bloomington: Indiana University Press, 2003), 184.

72   Leder, *My Life in Stalinist Russia*, 302.

73   Richard Lentz and Karla K. Gower, *The Opinions of Mankind: Racial Issues, Press, and Propaganda in the Cold War* (Columbia, MO: University of Missouri Press, 2010), 139; and Ann K. Johnson, *Urban Ghetto Riots, 1965-1968: A Comparison of Soviet and American Press Coverage* (Boulder, CO: East European Monographs, 1996), 22–37.

74   "Justice Is Asked for Minorities," *New York Times*, April 6, 1946.

75   Lentz and Gower, *The Opinions of Mankind*, 144–5; Johnson, *Urban Ghetto Riots,* 24; and Mary L. Dudziak, *Cold War Civil Rights: Race and the Image of American Democracy* (Princeton: Princeton University Press, 2000), 93.

76   Quoted in Dudziak, *Cold War Civil Rights*, 37, 38.

77   Quoted in Dudziak, *Cold War Civil Rights*, 38, 121.

78   "Soviet Media Coverage of Current US Racial Crisis," June 1963, Papers of John F. Kennedy, National Security Files, JFKNSF-295-016-p0002-p0006.

79   Eve Darian-Smith, "Re-Reading W. E. B. Du Bois: The Global Dimensions of the US Civil Rights Struggle," *Journal of Global History* 7, no. 3 (2012): 483–505.

80   Quoted in Lewis, *W. E. B. Du Bois*, 398.

81   W. E. B. Du Bois, "The Negro and the Warsaw Ghetto," in Herbert Aptheker, ed., *Writings by Du Bois in Periodicals Edited by Others*, vol. 4 (Millwood, NY: Kraus-Thompson, 1982), 175.

82   Du Bois, *Russia and America*, 256, 284.

83   "Interview with Dr. W. E. B. Du Bois by Al Morgan," June 4, 1957, p. 1, W. E. B. Du Bois Papers (MS 312), Special Collections and University Archives, University of Massachusetts Amherst Libraries.

84   Charles Stevenson, "No Passports for Our Enemies," 71; and "Letter from Harcourt, Brace, and Company to W. E. B. Du Bois," July 13, 1950, W. E. B. Du Bois Papers (MS 312), Special Collections and University Archives, University of Massachusetts Amherst Libraries. The files of the FBI are available under the Freedom of Information Act. https://va ult.fbi.gov/E.%20B.%20%28William%29%20Dubois.

85   Lewis, *W. E. B. Du Bois*, 560–1; and Shirley Graham Du Bois, "Account of The Asian-African Writers Conference, Tashkent, Uzbekistan, October 7-13, 1958," Special Collections and University

Archives, W. E. B. Du Bois Papers (MS 312), University of Massachusetts Amherst Libraries.

86 "Presentation of Lenin Peace Prize to Dr. William E. B. Du Bois," Embassy of the Union Soviet Socialist Republics, June 23, 1960, Special Collections and University Archives, W. E. B. Du Bois Papers (MS 312), University of Massachusetts Amherst Libraries.

87 Maxim Matusevich, "Soviet Antiracism and Its Discontents: The Cold War Years," in *Alternative Globalizations: Eastern Europe and the Postcolonial World*, ed. James Mark, Artemy M. Kalinovsky, and Steffi Marung (Bloomington: Indiana University Press, 2020), 238; and Djagalov, *From Internationalism to Postcolonialism*, 73.

88 Constantin Katsakioris, "Burden or Allies? Third World Students and Internationalist Duty through Soviet Eyes," *Kritika: Explorations in Russian and Eurasian History* 18, no. 3 (2017): 539–67.

89 Jan Carew, *Green Winter: A Novel About a Negro Student in Moscow Today* (New York: Stein and Day, 1965). See also Julie Hessler, "Death of an African Student in Moscow: Race, Politics, and the Cold War," *Cahiers du monde russe* 47, no. 1–2 (2006): 33–64; and Anika Walke, "Was Soviet Internationalism Anti-Racist? Toward a History of Foreign Others in the USSR," *Ideologies of Race*, 302–3.

90 Quoted in Matusevich, "Soviet Antiracism and Its Discontents," 243.

91 Hessler, "Death of an African Student in Moscow."

92 Jeff Sahadeo, *Voices from the Edge: Southern Migrants in Leningrad and Moscow* (Ithaca, NY: Cornell University Press, 2019), 93–115.

93 W. E. B. Du Bois, "Color Line," *The National Guardian*, December 3, 1952, W. E. B. Du Bois Papers (MS 312), Special Collections and University Archives, University of Massachusetts Amherst Libraries.

Chapter 4

1 Daniel Treisman, "Inequality: The Russian Experience," *Current History* 111, no. 747 (2012): 264–9; and Andrei Shleifer and Daniel Treisman, "A Normal Country: Russia After Communism," *Journal of Economic Perspectives* 19, no. 1 (2005): 151–74. See also Serguei Oushakine, *Patriotism of Despair: Nation, War, and Loss in Russia* (Ithaca, NY: Cornell University Press, 2009).

2 Jule DaVanzo and Clifford Grammich, *Dire Demographics: Population Trends in the Russian Federation* (Santa Monica, CA: RAND, 2001), 1–9, 40–1; and Ekaterina Selezneva and Tatiana Karabchuk, "Fertility

and Uncertainty in Modern Russia," in *Demography of Russia: From the Past to the Present*, ed. Tatiana Karabchuk, Kazuhiro Kumo, and Ekaterina Selezneva (London: Palgrave Macmillan, 2017), 155–85; and Marlene Laruelle and Jean Radvanyi, *Understanding Russia: The Challenges of Transformation* (New York: Rowman & Littlefield, 2019), 34.

3   Quoted in Michele A. Parsons, *Dying Unneeded: The Cultural Context of the Russian Mortality Crisis* (Nashville, TN: Vanderbilt University Press, 2014), 2.

4   Vladimir Putin's annual address to the Federal Assembly of the Russian Federation, July 8, 2000. http://en.kremlin.ru/events/president/transcri pts/21480. See also DaVanzo and Grammich, *Dire Demographics*, 1–9.

5   Paul Globe, "2010 Census Shows Fewer Russians, More Non-Russians, and Many Who No Longer Declare an Ethnic Identity At All," *Eurasia Daily Monitor* 9, issue 223 (2012). https://jamestown.org/program/ 2010-census-shows-fewer-russians-more-non-russians-and-many-who -no-longer-declare-an-ethnic-identity-at-all/.

6   I borrow the phrase from Anne Case and Angus Deaton, *Deaths of Despair and the Future of Capitalism* (Princeton: Princeton University Press, 2020), which analyzes the troubling rise of deaths of working-class white Americans in the twenty-first century.

7   Richard Arnold, *Russian Nationalism and Ethnic Violence: Symbolic Violence, Lynching, Pogrom, and Massacre* (London: Routledge, 2016), 16.

8   Arnold, *Russian Nationalism and Ethnic Violence*, 1–30; and Johannes Due Enstad, "Right-Wing Terrorism and Violence in Putin's Russia," *Terrorism Research Initiative* 12, no. 6 (2018): 90. For the broader context, see Holzer, Martin Laryš, and Miroslav Mareš, *Militant Right-Wing Extremism in Putin's Russia: Legacies, Forms, and Threats* (London: Routledge, 2018).

9   Recent research has shown that, contrary to accepted wisdom, higher xenophobic sentiment is linked to a lack of confidence in Putin's regime. See Hannah S. Chapman, Kyle L. Marquardt, Yoshiko M. Herrera, and Theodore P. Gerber, "Xenophobia on the Rise? Temporal and Regional Trends in Xenophobic Attitudes in Russia," *Comparative Politics* 50, no. 3 (2018): 381–94.

10 Doudou Diène, "Report of the Special Rapporteur on Contemporary Forms of Racism, Discrimination, Xenophobia, and Related Intolerance," United Nations, May 30, 2007. https://digitallibrary.un .org/record/601017?ln=en. For a broader perspective, see Cynthia

Notes

Miller-Idriss, *Hate in the Homeland: The New Global Far Right* (Princeton: Princeton University Press, 2020), 143.

11 "Rise of a Skinhead: How Russia's White Supremacists are Trying to Build Their Own Prison Brotherhood," *Meduza*, December 28, 2018. https://meduza.io/en/feature/2018/12/28/rise-of-a-skinhead.

12 Charles Clover, "The Skinhead Terrorists," *Financial Times*, December 3, 2010. https://www.ft.com/content/21553438-fcda-11df-ae2d-00144feab 49a.

13 Clover, "The Skinhead Terrorists."

14 Due Enstad, "Right-Wing Terrorism and Violence in Putin's Russia," 96. For a highly relevant study of the white power movement in America, see Kathleen Belew, *Bringing the War Home: The White Power Movement and Paramilitary America* (Cambridge, MA: Harvard University Press, 2018), esp. 1–16.

15 Vadim Rossman, *Russian Intellectual Antisemitism in the Post-Communist Era* (Lincoln: University of Nebraska Press, 2002), 4–5; and Neil MacMaster, *Racism in Europe, 1870-2000* (London: Palgrave, 2001), 207.

16 Due Enstad, "Right-Wing Terrorism and Violence in Putin's Russia," 90; and Clover, "The Skinhead Terrorists."

17 *Russian Federation: Violent Racism Out of Control, Amnesty International*, May 3, 2006, 1. https://www.amnesty.org/en/documents/ EUR46/022/2006/en/.

18 Quoted in Ulrika Ziemer, "Minority Youth, Everyday Racism, and Public Spaces in Contemporary Russia," *European Journal of Cultural Studies* 14, no. 2 (2011): 239. Translation slightly altered.

19 *"Dokumenty!" Discrimination on Grounds of Race in the Russian Federation* (London: Amnesty International Publications, 2003), 1–2.

20 "Russian Federation: Appeal Case—Khursheda Sultanova," *Amnesty International*, May 31, 2004. https://www.amnesty.org/en/document s/EUR46/022/2004/en/; and "Assassination of Mr. Samba Lampsar," *International Federation for Human Rights*, October 4, 2006. https:// www.fidh.org/en/region/europe-central-asia/russia/Assassination-of-Mr-Samba-Lampsar; and *Russian Federation: Violent Racism Out of Control*, 1.

21 Diène, "Report of the Special Rapporteur on Contemporary Forms of Racism," 2, 12, 15, 17.

22 "Rise of a Skinhead."

23   For a recent collection that traces the cross-fertilization between the European Far Right and Russia, see Melene Laruelle, ed., *Entangled Far Rights: A Russian-European Intellectual Romance in the Twentieth Century* (Pittsburgh: Pittsburgh University Press, 2018).

24   *"Dokumenty!"* 1.

25   UN Racism Official Concludes Inspection Tour," *Radio Free Europe*, June 16, 2006. https://www.rferl.org/a/1069237.html.

26   *Russian Federation: Violent Racism Out of Control*, 3.

27   Laruelle and Radvanyi, *Understanding Russia*, 23–5.

28   Valerie Sperling, *Sex, Politics & Putin: Political Legitimacy in Russia* (New York: Oxford University Press, 2015), 32–3; and Steven Lee Myers, *The New Tsar: The Rise and Reign of Vladimir Putin* (New York: Vintage Books, 2014), 159.

29   Quoted in Emma Gilligan, *Terror in Chechnya: Russia and the Tragedy of Civilians in War* (Princeton: Princeton University Press, 2010), 33.

30   Gilligan, *Terror in Chechnya*, 2.

31   Matthew Light, *Fragile Migration Rights: Freedom of Movement in Post-Soviet Russia* (New York: Routledge, 2016), 46–54.

32   On post-Soviet migration, see Laruelle and Radvanyi, *Understanding Russia*, 26–9; and Andrei V. Korobkov, "Post-Soviet Migration: New Trends at the Beginning of the Twenty-First Century," in *Migration, Homeland, and Belonging in* Eurasia, ed. Cynthia J. Buckley and Blaire Ruble, with Erin Trouth Hofmann (Washington, DC: Woodrow Wilson Center Press, 2008), 69.

33   On the problem of labeling, see Ziemer, "Minority Youth, Everyday Racism, and Public Spaces in Contemporary Russia," 236; and Alaina Lemon, *Between Two Fires: Gypsy Performance and Romani Memory from Pushkin to Postsocialism* (Durham: Duke University Press, 2000), 75.

34   Vladimir Putin's annual address to the Russian Federal Assembly, May 10, 2006, http://en.kremlin.ru/events/president/transcripts/23577.

35   *Implementation of the International Convention on the Elimination of All Forms of Racial Discrimination by the Russian Federation* (2013), 20–1. https://tbinternet.ohchr.org/Treaties/CERD/Shared%20Documents/RUS/INT_CERD_NGO_RUS_13735_E.pdf.

36   Quoted in Tiina Sotkasiira, *Russian Borderlands in Change: North Caucasian Youth and the Politics of Bordering and Citizenship* (New York: Routledge, 2016), 90–2; and Tatiana Rabinovich, "Anti-Muslim Racism in Russia" (unpublished manuscript).

37   *Implementation of the International Convention*, 20.

38   Stephen Hutchings and Vera Tolz, *Nation, Ethnicity, and Race on Russian Television: Mediating Post-Soviet Difference* (London: Routledge, 2015), 99, 112.

39   "Nationalist Uprising in Moscow has Serious Implications for the North Caucasus," *Eurasia Daily Monitor*, vol. 7, issue 224, December 15, 2010. https://www.refworld.org/docid/4d09ee892.html. For a highly edited video clip, see https://www.youtube.com/watch?v=y5Si05KCNYg.

40   Nikolay Zakharov, *Race and Racism in Russia* (London: Palgrave Macmillan, 2015), 122–3.

41   "The Phantom of Manezhnaya Square: Radical Nationalism and Efforts to Counteract It in 2010," Sova Center. https://www.sova-center.ru/en/ xenophobia/reports-analyses/2011/05/d21561/; and Hutchings and Tolz, *Nation, Ethnicity, and Race on Russian Television*, 97–115.

42   Jens Siegert, "Natives, Foreigners, and Native Foreigners—the Difficult Task of Coexistence in Russia," *Russian Analytical Digest* 141 (December 23, 2013): 8.

43   "Vladimir Putin Inaugurated as Russian President amid Moscow Protests," *The Guardian*, May 7, 2012, https://www.theguardian.com/wo rld/2012/may/07/vladimir-putin-inaugurated-russian-president.

44   Samuel A. Greene, *Moscow in Movement: Power and Opposition in Putin's Russia* (Stanford: Stanford University Press, 2014), 216. See also "Putin Takes Helm as Police Punish Dissent," *The New York Times*, May 7, 2012.

45   Annual Report of Racism and Xenophobia, Sova Center, 2012. https:// www.sova-center.ru/en/xenophobia/reports-analyses/2013/04/d26972/.

46   Andrey Makarychev and Sergei Medvedev, "Biopolitics and Power in Putin's Russia," *Problems of Post-Communism* 62, no. 1 (2015): 45–54.

47   Yoshiko M. Herrera and Nicole M. Butkovich Kraus, "Pride Versus Prejudice: Ethnicity, National Identity, and Xenophobia in Russia," *Comparative Politics* 48, no. 3 (2016): 293–312; Alexey Bessudnov and Andrey Shcherbak, "Ethnic Discrimination in Multi-Ethnic Societies: Evidence from Russia," *European Sociological Review* 36, no. 1 (2020): 104–20; and Eliot Borenstein, *Meanwhile, in Russia: Russian Internet Memes and Viral Video* (London: Bloomsbury, 2022).

48   "One Man's Fight Against Slavs-Only Apartment Rentals in Moscow," *The Moscow Times*, February 27, 2018. https://www.themoscowtimes .com/2018/02/27/one-man-pushes-back-against-slavs-only-renting-d iscrimination-a60632.

49 See Aleksandr Borodo's open letter, June 10, 2020. https://www.jewish -museum.ru/news/otkrytoe-pismo-generalnogo-direktora-evreyskogo -muzeya-i-tsentra-tolerantnosti-ravvina-aleksandra-bo/.

50 "Chem deshevle kvartira na rynke arendy zhil'ia v Rosii, tem slozhnee ee sniat' 'ne slavianam,'" *Novaia gazeta*, August 7, 2019. https://novayag azeta.ru/articles/2019/08/07/81525-slavyanskoe-gnezdo.

51 "Chem deshevle kvartira na rynke arendy zhil'ia v Rosii, tem slozhnee ee sniat' 'ne slavianam,'" and "Rassmotrim slavian," https://medium .com/@robustory. See also "Moscow's Most Racist Landlords Revealed," *The Moscow Times*, June 21, 2017. https://www.themoscowtimes.com /2017/06/21/new-research-reveals-moscows-most-racist-landlords-a5 8240.

52 "One Man's Fight Against Slavs-Only Apartment Rentals in Moscow."

53 "One Man's Fight Against Slavs-Only Apartment Rentals in Moscow."

54 Yandex Group Chat Forum, January 24, 2020. https://yandex.ru/q/quest ion/home/pochemu_v_rossii_priniato_pisat_chto_chto_286d993b/.

55 "Tol'ko slavianam: Diskriminatsiia v Rossii est', no dokazat' ee v sude pochti nevozmozhno," *Meduza*, June 11, 2018. https://meduza.io/feature /2018/06/11/tolko-slavyanam.

56 For the phrase "web of discrimination," see George Lipsitz, *The Possessive Investment in Whiteness: How White People Profit from Identity Politics,* rev. ed. (Philadelphia: Temple University Press, 2018), xvii. For comparisons with South Africa, see George M. Frederickson, *White Supremacy: A Comparative Study in American and South African History* (New York: Oxford University Press, 1981), 132.

57 David Brandenberger, *National Bolshevism: Stalinist Mass Culture and the Formation of Modern Russian National Identity, 1931-1956* (Cambridge, MA: Harvard University Press, 2002), 238–9, 246–7.

58 Kesha Fikes and Alaina Lemon, "African Presence in Former Spaces," *Annual Review of Anthropology* 31 (2002): 507, 517; and Zakharov, *Race and Racism in Russia*, 6.

SELECTED BIBLIOGRAPHY

Alexandrov, Vladimir. *Black Russian*. New York: Atlantic Monthly Press, 2013.

Arnold, Richard. *Russian Nationalism and Ethnic Violence: Symbolic Violence, Lynching, Pogrom, and Massacre*. London: Routledge, 2016.

Avrutin, Eugene M. *Jews and the Imperial State: Identification Politics in Tsarist Russia*. Ithaca, NY: Cornell University Press, 2010.

Baldwin, Kate A. *Beyond the Color Line and the Iron Curtain: Reading Encounters between Black and Red, 1922–1963*. Durham, NC: Duke University Press, 2002.

Bojanowska, Edyta M. *A World of Empires: The Russian Voyage of the Frigate Pallada*. Cambridge, MA: Harvard University Press, 2018.

Brown, Kate. *A Biography of No Place: From Ethnic Borderland to Soviet Heartland*. Cambridge, MA: Harvard University Press, 2004.

Carew, Joy Gleason. *Blacks, Reds, and Russians: Sojourners in Search of a Soviet Promise*. New Brunswick, NJ: Rutgers University Press, 2010.

Djagalov, Rossen. *From Internationalism to Postcolonialism: Literature and Cinema between the Second and the Third Worlds*. Montreal, QC: McGill-Queen's University Press, 2020.

Dudziak, Mary L. *Cold War Civil Rights: Race and the Image of American Democracy*. Princeton, NJ: Princeton University Press, 2000.

Due Enstad, Johannes. "Right-Wing Terrorism and Violence in Putin's Russia." *Terrorism Research Initiative* 12, no. 6 (2018): 89–103.

Engelstein, Laura. *The Keys to Happiness: Sex and the Search for Modernity in Fin-de-Siècle Russia*. Ithaca, NY: Cornell University Press, 1992.

Etkind, Alexander. *Internal Colonization: Russia's Imperial Experience*. Cambridge: Polity, 2011.

Gilbert, George. *The Radical Right in Late Imperial Russia: Dreams of a True Fatherland?* London: Routledge, 2016.

Gilligan, Emma. *Terror in Chechnya: Russia and the Tragedy of Civilians in War*. Princeton, NJ: Princeton University Press, 2010.

Glaser, Amelia M. and Steven S. Lee, eds. *Comintern Aesthetics*. Toronto. ON: University of Toronto Press, 2020.

Hessler, Julie. "Death of an African Student in Moscow: Race, Politics, and the Cold War." *Cahiers du monde russe* 47, no. 1–2 (2006): 33–64.

Hillis, Faith. *Children of Rus': Right-Bank Ukraine and the Invention of a Russian Nation*. Ithaca, NY: Cornell University Press, 2013.

Hirsch, Francine. *Empire of Nations: Ethnographic Knowledge and the Making of the Soviet Union*. Ithaca, NY: Cornell University Press, 2005.

Hsu, Chia Yin. "A Tale of Two Railroads: 'Yellow Labor', Agrarian Colonization, and the Making of Russianness at the Far Eastern Frontier, 1890s-1910s." *Ab Imperio* 3 (2006): 217–53.

Hutchings, Stephen and Vera Tolz, *Nation, Ethnicity, and Race on Russian Television: Mediating Post-Soviet Difference*. London: Routledge, 2015.

Kiaer, Christina, "African Americans in Soviet Socialist Realism: The Case of Aleksandr Deineka." *The Russian Review* 75, no. 3 (2016): 402–33.

Kolchin, Peter. *Unfree Labor: American Slavery and Russian Serfdom*. Cambridge, MA: Harvard University Press, 1987.

Laruelle, Marlene, ed. *Entangled Far Rights: A Russian-European Intellectual Romance in the Twentieth Century*. Pittsburgh, PA: Pittsburgh University Press, 2018.

Lee, Steven S. *The Ethnic Avant-Garde: Minority Cultures and World Revolution*. New York: Columbia University Press, 2015.

Lemon, Alaina. *Between Two Fires: Gypsy Performance and Romani Memory from Pushkin to Postsocialism*. Durham, NC: Duke University Press, 2000.

Light, Matthew. *Fragile Migration Rights: Freedom of Movement in Post-Soviet Russia*. New York: Routledge, 2016.

Lohr, Eric. *Nationalizing the Russian Empire: The Campaign against Enemy Aliens during World War I*. Cambridge, MA: Harvard University Press, 2003.

Matusevich, Maxim. "Soviet Antiracism and Its Discontents: The Cold War Years." In *Alternative Globalizations: Eastern Europe and the Postcolonial World*, ed. James Mark, Artemy M. Kalinovsky, and Steffi Marung, 229–50. Bloomington, IN: Indiana University Press, 2020.

McGeever, Brendan. *Antisemitism and the Russian Revolution*. Cambridge, MA: Cambridge University Press, 2019.

Mogilner, Marina. *Homo Imperii: A History of Physical Anthropology in Russia*. Lincoln, NE: University of Nebraska Press, 2013.

Park, Alyssa M. *Sovereignty Experiments: Korean Migrants and the Building of Borders in Northeast Asia, 1860-1945*. Ithaca, NY: Cornell University Press, 2019.

Rainbow, David, ed. *Ideologies of Race: Imperial Russia and the Soviet Union in Global Context*. Montreal, QC: McGill-Queen's University Press, 2019.

Rogger, Hans. *Jewish Policies and Right-Wing Politics in Imperial Russia*. Berkeley, CA: University of California Press, 1986.

Selected Bibliography

Roman, Meredith L. *Opposing Jim Crow: African Americans and the Soviet Indictment of U.S. Racism, 1928–1937*. Lincoln, NE: University of Nebraska Press, 2012.

Sahadeo, Jeff. *Voices from the Soviet Edge: Southern Migrants in Leningrad and Moscow*. Ithaca, NY: Cornell University Press, 2019.

Shearer, David. "Elements Near and Alien: Passportization, Policing, and Identity in the Stalinist State." *Journal of Modern History* 76, no. 4 (2004): 835–81.

Siegelbaum, Lewis H. "Another 'Yellow Peril': Chinese Migrants in the Russian Far East and the Russian Reaction before 1917." *Modern Asian Studies* 12, no. 2 (1978): 307–30.

Sloin, Andrew. *The Jewish Revolution in Belorussia: Economy, Race, and Bolshevik Power*. Bloomington, IN: Indiana University Press, 2017.

Sotkasiira, Tiina. *Russian Borderlands in Change: North Caucasian Youth and the Politics of Bordering and Citizenship*. New York: Routledge, 2016.

Sunderland, Willard. *The Baron's Cloak: A History of the Russian Empire in War and Revolution*. Ithaca, NY: Cornell University Press, 2014.

Urbansky, Sören. *Beyond the Steppe Frontier: A History of the Sino-Russian Border*. Princeton, NJ: Princeton University Press, 2020.

Uy, Michael, "Performing Catfish Row in the Soviet Union: The Everyman Opera Company and *Porgy and Bess*, 1955–1956." *Journal of the Society of American Music* 11, no. 4 (2017): 470–501.

Weinberg, Robert. *Blood Libel in Late Imperial Russia: The Ritual Murder Trial of Mendel Beilis*. Bloomington, IN: Indiana University Press, 2014.

Zakharov, Nikolay. *Race and Racism in Russia*. London: Palgrave Macmillan, 2015.

INDEX

Index

Index